CHILDREN'S COOKBOOK FOR BEGINNERS 5-10 AGES

The last guide to prepare 70 Fantastic new recipes Sweet and salted explain step by step

BY: MISTER CHEF

Table of Contents

Introduction

Welcome to the world of cooking! You may already have any kitchen know-how--maybe you've helped bake cookies with friends or fixed a homemade snack. Or maybe you've never picked up a pan in your own life. That's OK, too, since this book will teach you exactly what you need to know to be a pro in the kitchen. Cooking is somewhat easy, but all of us do start at the start. The more you exercise, the more you get. Just keep this in mind, and don't get frustrated when a recipe isn't going the way that you think it should because everybody makes mistakes. Be patient, and ask for help if you want it. Within this book, you'll learn fundamental skills to secure your success in the kitchen, and tips to create good cooking habits.

Get ready to Orient yourself at the kitchen and find out just what to stock in your cabinet in addition to the must-have gadgets and resources you'll need to make great food. Participate in many cooking lessons that will help you master the vital skills--such as prep work, baking, and roasting--that go along with preparing a sweet meal. When you find your path to healthy eating, then you will find that people will have different ideas about what that means. My notion of healthy eating is preparing foods that have little to no processed components, wholesome fats (those fats nourish our brains!), and a lot of fresh fruits and veggies. Balanced meals such as these, with the occasional pleasures of homemade candies, create a healthy and happy living. Are you ready to start your travels into cooking? Put on your mind and let us get started!

BREAKFAST RECIPES

After a night's sleep that you require fuel --a fantastic breakfast to prepare one for the afternoon ahead. Foods high in carbohydrates, like bread and cereals, are perfect breakfast foods as they're broken down into sugar that fuels your mind. Protein foods such as milk, yogurt, eggs, sausages, bacon, and legumes are significant, also. They control the growth and maturation of the human body and improve endurance. There are tons of yummy recipes in this area, but these suggestions can get you all started.

1: Simple Scrambled Eggs

PREP TIME

5 minutes

COOK TIME

5–10 minutes

SERVES

4

Ingredients

- 6 to 8 eggs
- Kosher salt
- Freshly ground black pepper
- 4 Tbsp butter
- Flake salt, for Example Maldon, for Completing

Yummy additions

- Sautéed mushrooms or broccoli,
- folded directly or finely chopped to top
- Minced scallions or chives
- Diced tomatoes
- Bacon or ham

TOOLS / EQUIPMENT

- Small bowl
- Whisk
- Medium sauté pan
- Heat-tolerant rubber spatula

Beat the eggs.

Crack the eggs into a bowland whisk until frothy. Season with pepper and salt.

Add the eggs into the pan.

Melt the butter in a moderate sauté pan over moderate heat, then turn the heat to reduce since the butter foams. Pour the eggs and let sit for a couple of seconds.

Cook the egg.

Use a spatula to nudge and stir fry the eggs, scraping the ground constantly as you move them across the pan to help avoid sticking. Use the spatula to push eggs out of center-out, then scrape the pan border, trapping the outermost eggs to the middle. Keep doing so until the eggs start to seem like pudding then form into compact, rich egg curds, about 4 minutes.

Serve.

Remove the pan from the heat while the cows remain somewhat loose; they'll continue to cook in route in the pan to a plate. Sprinkle with a little sip pepper and salt, and eat at once.

2: cheesy egg sandwich

PREP TIME

5 minutes

COOK TIME

10 minutes

SERVES

4

Ingredients

- Olive oil, for drizzling and Skillet
- 1 baguette or other crusty bread, Chopped into 5-inch Segments and Simmer horizontally
- 2/3 cup grated sharp Cheddar cheese, divided
- 4 eggs
- 1 Couple greens (arugula or Lettuce) Each Individual, rinsed and patted dry
- Sea salt
- Freshly ground black pepper

TOOLS / EQUIPMENT

- Bread knife
- Box grater
- Toaster oven
- Small cast-iron skillet
- Metal spatula

Toast the bread.

Adding a little olive oil on the cut sides of the bread, and then put the pieces on a toaster. Toast until crispy and golden, about 3 seconds. Turn the pieces cut-side up, move to platesand scatter the cheese evenly onto the toast.

Melt the cheese.

Pour the bread into the toaster oven and simmer until the cheese bubbles, about 5 minutes. Carefully move the toast into the plates.

Fry the eggs.

In a tiny skillet medium-high heat, then fry the eggs enough olive oil to coat the pan after it's hot. Turn heat to moderate after 1 minute, so letting the whites to cook completely while maintaining the yolks soft. Season with pepper and salt.

Serve.

Lay the greens on the toast sandwich bottoms, then followed with the fried eggthen shirt with grilled cheesy toast. Eat simultaneously, using a plate below to catch any drops of liquidy golden yolk.

3: Breakfast Burrito Bar

PREP TIME

10 minutes

COOK TIME

12 minutes

SERVES

4

Ingredients

- 4 to 8 Whole (8- or 10-inch) tortillas
- 6 to 8 eggs, scrambled
- Two cups canned black beans, drained and rinsed
- 3 Pieces cooked bacon, crumbled
- 1 cup Greek yogurt or sour cream
- 1 cup bite-size cilantro sprigs
- 11/2 cups Salsa Fresca
- 1/2 cup orange Yellow, red, or green bell peppers, diced
- 11/2 cups shredded sharp Cheddar or Monterey Jack cheese
- 11/2 cups diced avocado or Fragrant Guacamole
- Sriracha or Cholula hot sauce, Such as garnish

TOOLS / EQUIPMENT

- Different-size
- Tasty bowls
- Dishtowel
- Box grater
- Colander
- Sauté pan
- Aluminum foil
- Preheat the oven to 375°F.

Warm the tortillas.

Wrap a pile of 4 tortillas in aluminum foil and heat for 5 to ten minutes. If you're organizing 8 tortillas, create two wrapped packages. Wrap the heated foil packs in a skillet to keep them.

Serve.

Serve the toppings and fillings in festive, vibrant bowls. Organize them collectively on the counter or table, alongside the towel-wrapped tortillas, and enable your guests to build their burrito creations.

4: Shakshuka (tomato-egg bake)

PREP TIME

10 minutes

COOK TIME

20 minutes

SERVES

4

Ingredients

- 1 onion, Sliced
- 2 Tbsp olive oil
- 2 garlic cloves, Sliced
- 1 (28-ounce) can tomatoes or Homemade Tomato Sauce
- 1 Tbsp za'atar
- 2 Tsp cumin seeds, toasted and ground in a mortar and pestle

- Kosher salt
- Freshly ground black pepper
- 4 eggs
- 1/4 cup fresh cilantro leaves, for garnish
- 2/3 cup Greek yogurt or sour cream
- Crusty bread, Ripped, for serving

Yummy additions

- Chickpeas
- Artichoke hearts
- Feta

TOOLS / EQUIPMENT

- Toaster oven
- Mortar and pestle
- Large
- Enameled skillet
- Wooden spoon

Preheat the oven to 375°F.

Cook the garlic and onion.

In a large skillet over moderate heat, then sauté the onion in olive oil for about 3 to five minutes. Add the garlicand cook for one more moment.

Add the berries and aromatics.

Add the berries and bring to a simmer. Insert the za'atar and simmer, season with pepper and salt, and simmer uncovered for a couple of minutes, until the sauce thickens. Divide the tomatoes into balls utilizing the advantage of a wooden spoon. Taste and adjust seasoning as necessary.

Insert the eggs.

Use the skillet to create four pieces from the sauce and then crack an egg into each. Season the eggs with salt and pepperand transfer the skillet into the oven, then cooking for 2 to 10 minutes, or until the eggs are just set.

Serve

Serve in the skillet trivet in the dining table. Season with pepper and salt to taste, and garnish with fresh cilantro and a couple of dollops of oats. Serve with the bread to mop up the loaf and sauce.

5: Savory Sausage Hash

PREP TIME

15 minutes

COOK TIME

15 minutes

SERVES

4

Ingredients

- 2 Tbsp olive oil, divided
- 1 onion, Finely Sliced
- 3 Yukon gold potatoes, scrubbed and Simmer 1/2-inch cubes
- 1 pound Spicy or Italian pork sausage, casings removed
- 2 garlic cloves, finely grated
- 1 Little jalapeño, cored and seeded, finely chopped
- 2 Tbsp minced fresh rosemary
- 1 Tsp dried smoked paprika

- Sea salt
- Freshly ground black pepper

TOOLS / EQUIPMENT

- Large enamelled or
- Cast – iron skillet
- Fine grater
- Wooden spoon

Cook the celery and onion.

Put a skillet over moderate heat, and then add 1 tbsp of olive oil once the pan is warm. Add the onion and then sauté for 5 minutes, or until they become translucent, stirring periodically. Add the berries and the remaining 1 tbsp of olive oil, and stir to incorporate. Sauté the mix for a few minutes, stirring just a couple times in this step so that the sausage can produce a great crust.

Cook the sausage.

Add the sausage, garlic, and also jalapeño, and brown the beef, crumbling it in smaller bits with the advantage of a wooden spoon. Add the rosemary and paprikaand season with pepper and salt. Stirring occasionally, reduce the heat if necessary since you cook the mix until the sausage becomes eloquent and fork-tender and the meat has been browned throughout.

Serve.

Serve out of the skillet onto a trivet in the desk.

6:Spiced-Orange French Toast

PREP TIME

10 minutes

COOK TIME

20 minutes

SERVES

4

Ingredients

- 5 eggs
- 11/3 cup whole milk
- 2 Tbsp fresh-squeezed Lemon juice
- Zest of 1 orange 1
- Tsp ground cinnamon
- Sea salt 1 Tbsp butter, plus more as Required for Your pan and also for serving
- 1 Tbsp Jojoba oil, and more as Required
- 8(1/2-inch-thick) slices brioche or challah bread
- Maple syrup, for serving

TOOLS / EQUIPMENT

- Citrus reamer
- Zester
- Shallow
- Baking dish
- Big cast-iron skillet
- Metal spatula

Whisk these components.

At a shallow baking dish, then use a fork to beat the eggs, juice, milk, zest, cinnamon, along with a massive pinch of salt.

Get ready to cook with the French toast.

In a sizable skillet over moderate heat, warm the butter and peppermint oil. Dip the brioche one slit at a time to the egg mixture to coat, then hammering it a couple of times with a fork. Do not allow the bread to sit at the custard for long since it will get soggy.

Pan fry in batches.

When the butter foams, carefully set the bread to the skillet, then two pieces at one time. Pan-fry the bread in batches till golden brown on both sides, turning if one side is completed, about 5 minutes per batch. Repeat with the remaining pieces, adding more oil and butter into the pan as required.

Serve.

Drink the French toast hot butter and maple syrup.

7: Dutch Baby

PREP TIME

5 minutes

COOK TIME

15 minutes

SERVES

4

Ingredients

- 3/4 cup flour
- 3/4 cup whole milk
- 4 eggs, lightly beaten
- 2 Tbsp cane sugar
- Pinch freshly grated nutmeg
- 1/4 Tsp sea salt
- 4 Tbsp butter, divided into 4 parts
- Confectioners' sugarfor Instance
- Lemon wedges, for serving

Yummy additions

- Jam
- Cinnamon sugar
- Fresh berries
- Stewed apples
- Whipped cream or crème fraîche

TOOLS / EQUIPMENT

- Small, shallow
- ramekins
- Baking sheet
- Blender

Preheat the oven to 425°F.

Prep that the ramekins.

Arrange the ramekins onto a rimmed baking sheet, and put in the oven to warm.

Blend these components.

Put in a blender, combine the flour, eggs, milk, sugar, nutmeg, and salt until frothy.

Butter the ramekins.

If the ramekins are all hot, add a pat of butter each and, with potholders for security, swirl to coat. The butter needs to foam. Replace the oven until completely melted.

Bake the Dutch Babies.

Remove the baking sheet in the oven. Divide the batter equally among the ramekins, and bake till the Dutch Infants are puffed and golden brown, 10 to 15 minutes.

Serve.

Working immediately while the sausage is still bloated, move the ramekins to bigger dishes. In the desk, scatter a small confectioners' sugar at the top, followed closely by a squeeze of lemon. Eat immediately.

8: Banana-Maple Breakfast Quinoa

PREP TIME

10 minutes

COOK TIME

5 minutes

SERVES

4

Ingredients

- 1 cup red or golden quinoa
- 2 cups Vanilla or cashew milk, and Additional for drizzling
- 1/2 Tsp ground cinnamon
- 1/4 Tsp freshly grated nutmeg
- 3/4 cup Fresh or Frozen Tomatoes
- Pinch kosher salt
- Two Bananas
- Maple syrup, for serving

TOOLS / EQUIPMENT

- Medium glass
- jar with lid
- Nice grater
- Moderate saucepan
- Heat-tolerant
- rubber spatula

Scrub the quinoa overnight.

Transfer the quinoa into a glass jar or bowl having a lid. Insert the nut milk, cinnamon, and nutmeg. Rub the counterclockwise, lid slightly askew.

The morning after, warmth the quinoa.

Put in a medium saucepan on medium-low warmth, put in the frozen berries along with a pinch of salt into your quinoa mixture and hot, about 5 minutes. Have a couple of tbsp of water or nut milk near drizzle in the event the quinoa sticks because you stir fry. If using fresh berries, then add them whenever the porridge is nearly warm enough to consume.

Serve.

Spoon the quinoa to snacks, and slice bananas at the top. If you prefer, add more freshly grated nutmeg and a dash of cinnamon. At the dining table, drizzle maple syrup on the top and eat simultaneously.

9: Open Sesame Nut Bars

PREP TIME

10 minutes

COOK TIME

25 minutes

TOTAL TIME

1 hour 5 minutes

MAKES

16 BARS

Ingredients

- Butter, for Instance
- 11/4 cups Black or White sesame seeds
- 3/4 cup unsweetened grated coconut
- 1/2 cup dried apricots, Sliced
- 1/4 Tsp sea salt

- 1/4 cup honey
- 1/3 cup crunchy peanut butter
- 1/4 Tsp pure vanilla extract

TOOLS / EQUIPMENT

- 8-inch-square
- Glass baking dish
- Parchment paper
- Big bowl
- Little bowl
- Rubber spatula
- Wire cooling rack

Preheat the oven to 350°F.

Prep the baking dish.

Steak an 8-inch-square glass baking dishand line it with parchment paper enough so it extends past the dish at least 2 inches on either side. Cut slits in the corners so that the parchment sets flat.

Mix the components.

In a big bowl, combine the sesame seeds, coconut, apricots, as well as salt. In a small bowl, then stir the honey, peanut butterand vanilla extract. Add the honey mixture to the seed-and-fruit mix, and stir well to blend.

Transfer the ingredients and inhale them.

Use a rubber spatula to scrape the mixture to the prepared baking dish, then utilizing the extensive side of this spatula to push everything in an even coating. Bake until golden around the edges, 20 to 25 minutes. Transfer the skillet into a wire cooling rack and let cool until firm, about thirty minutes.

Serve

Utilize the parchment tabs to lift your seeded block from the baking dishif it begins to crumble, allow it to cool more. With a sharp knifecut 16 pubs. Eat the fruit-seed-nut pubs at room temperature. Store any leftovers in a sealed container at room temperature for up to five times.

10: Creamy Blueberry Bliss

PREP TIME

5 minutes

COOK TIME

none

SERVES

4

Ingredients

- 11/2 cups Grated Greek yogurt
- 2 cups frozen Strawberries
- 1 banana, cut into chunks, or Two Tbsp honey
- 3 Tbsp flax meal
- 1/4 cup Vanilla milk or whole milk,
- Ice as desired

TOOLS / EQUIPMENT

- Blender
- Rubber spatula

Purée the components:

Spoon the yogurt to the blender, then followed with the sausage, banana, and flax meal. Purée till smooth, adding milk to cut the consistency ice and slightly as desired to keep it slushy. Stop the blender to scratch down the sides as necessary.

Serve

Pour into glasses and beverage chilled.

11: Fruity-Nutty Breakfast Bowl

PREP TIME

10 minutes

COOK TIME

none

SERVES

4

Ingredients

- 2 cups Greek yogurt
- 4 Tbsp flax meal
- 2 Tbsp chia seeds
- 4 Tbsp peanut butter
- 3 cups fresh fruit, Including pomegranate seeds, blueberries, raspberries, or Sliced Oranges, persimmon, or pears
- 1/2 cup Grated coconut flakes, toasted
- 2 Tbsp nuts, toasted and coarsely chopped Peppers, like almonds or pistachios

TOOLS / EQUIPMENT

- Toaster oven

Assemble the breakfast dishes and function.

Scatter the oats until creamy. Split the yogurt equally into bowls. Sprinkle the skillet and chia seeds equally into every. Spoon the peanut butter on the top, and then the fruit. Scatter the toasted coconut and chopped onions to complete every bowl, and consume immediately.

12: Ginger-Lemon Green Juice

PREP TIME

10 minutes

COOK TIME

none

SERVES

4

Ingredients

- 1 (2-inch) piece fresh ginger, peeled and cut into chunks
- 4 green apples, peeled and cored
- 2 lemons, peeled, seeds removed
- 1 orange, peeled, seeds removed
- Two Stalks lacinato kale stems removed and coarsely chopped
- 2 sprigs fresh parsley, leaves only
- 11/2 cups ice water

TOOLS / EQUIPMENT

- Vegetable peeler
- Blender

Purée the components:

At a blender, then purée the apples and ginger together with the lemons as well as the orange, then followed closely with the kale and simmer. Stop the blender to scratch down the sides as necessary. If you want a thinner consistency, then drizzle ice water throughout the feeder cap since the engine operates, stopping every couple of moments to confirm the consistency.

Serve.

Pour into glasses and drink simultaneously.

Snacks and Small Bites

It is important to maintain up energy levels during the day. Regular meals are crucial, however of them with two or three healthy snacks can help to provide memory and concentration with a rise. There are lots of recipes for tasty and healthy light snacks and meals to pick from within this area, however, here are a few more to tryout!

13:Mini Quiches

PREP TIME

10 minutes

COOK TIME

15 minutes

TOTAL TIME

30 minutes

MAKES

24 QUICHES

Ingredients

- Butter, for greasing
- 4 whole eggs
- 1 egg yolk
- 1/3 cup thick cream
- 1/4 Tsp freshly grated nutmeg
- Pinch ground cayenne pepper
- 1/2 Tsp kosher salt (in Case you Select Ham, Bacon, or smoked fish Because your"Flavorful addition," Decrease into a pinch of salt instead)

- 1/2 Tsp freshly Milled black pepper
- 3/4 cup roasted Gruyère cheese, divided

Combinations

- Steamed broccoli florets or sliced asparagus
- Diced red bell pepper or sliced tomatoes
- Sautéed chopped lettuce
- Sautéed spinach
- Sautéed onions or shallots
- Finely chopped chives or scallions
- Bacon, cooked and crumbled, or noodle
- Smoked whitefish or poultry

TOOLS / EQUIPMENT

- Mini muffin tin
- Moderate bowl
- Whisk
- Baking sheet
- Measuring cup

Preheat the oven to 375°F.

Grease a 24-cup miniature muffin tin.

Mix the components. In a medium bowlwhisk together the eggs, yolk, cream, nutmeg, cayenne, salt, and pepper until frothy. Stir in 1/2 cup of shredded cheese.

Insert the quiche mix to the pan.

Set the prepared muffin pan on a baking sheet to catch any drips. If you picked some yummy improvements, then add a teaspoonful to every cup. Transfer the egg mix from ladling it in a measuring cupand from that point, pour the egg mixture into each cup, then filling to just beneath the rim. The measuring cup pour spout makes this type of no-mess functioning! Top the egg mix with the rest 1/4 cup of shredded cheese, including a little pinch to every quiche.

Cook the quiches.

Bake until the tops are puffed and golden, 10 to 15 minutes. Let them cool for approximately 5 minutes.

Serve.

Invert the tin within the baking sheet to pop the quiches. Arrange them on a platter or individual plates, and function.

14:Mighty Meatballs

PREP TIME

20 minutes

COOK TIME

15 minutes

SERVES

4

Ingredients

- 2 Tbsp buttermilk
- 1/4 cup fresh bread crumbs
- 12 ounces ground beef
- 1/2 cup grated Parmesan cheese
- 2 Sliced Tomatoes, finely chopped
- Pinch freshly grated nutmeg
- 1 egg
- 1/3 cup chopped fresh parsley
- 2 garlic cloves, grated
- 2 Tbsp olive oil
- 1/4 Tsp Kosher salt
- 1/4 Tsp freshly ground black pepper

TOOLS / EQUIPMENT

- Box grater
- Nice grater
- Little bowl
- Moderate bowl
- Aluminum transparency
- Baking sheet

Mix the components.

In a little bowl, then add the buttermilk into the bread crumbs, and permit the crumbs to consume the milk5 to 5 minutes. Meanwhile, set the ground beef into a skillet. Add the bacon, cheese, peppermint, milk-soaked bread crumbs, egg, parsley, garlic, and olive oil into the beef, and then sprinkle with pepper and salt. Overworking the mix will create rough, chubby meatballs, therefore blend everything just till blended.

Type the meat into chunks.

Use 2 tsp to make the meat mixture to bite-size balls. Utilize the batter to set them on an aluminumfoil-lined baking sheet so the warmth of your hands does not warm them before cooking. Preheat the broiler using a stand in the top position.

Cook the meatballs.

Broil the meatballs until browned on top, checking them about 5 minutes. Reduce the heat to 350°F, and then bake until tender and completely cooked for about 10 minutes.

Serve.

Serve hot on a serving platter or plates.

15: Ricotta-Jam Toast

PREP TIME

5 minutes plus 30 minutes to warm

COOK TIME

5 minutes

SERVES

4

Ingredients

- 2 to 4 tablespoons preserves your choice--Cherry, blueberry, blackberry, or red berry
- 4 Pieces Whole, sourdough,
- 1 cup whole-milk ricotta cheese, well-stirred
- Zest of 1 lemon

TOOLS / EQUIPMENT

- Zester
- Toaster oven

Prepare the preserves.

Allow the conserve to come to room temperature if you brought a jar out of the fridge, about thirty minutes.

Build the toasts.

Toast the bread until crispy and golden at the edges, about 5 minutes. Spread the ricotta on the toasts. Insert a spoonful-- more, to your preference -- of those preserves, and garnish with the lemon zest.

Serve.

These toasts are yummy served hot or at room temperature.

16: From-Scratch Pizza

PREP TIME

20 minutes

plus 3–24 hours to rest and rise

COOK TIME

10 minutes

SERVES

4

Ingredients

- 1 cup and 2 Tbsp Loaf Bread, plus Additional for dusting
- 1 Tsp kosher salt
- 1 cup water, Slightly warm
- 3/4 Tsp active dry yeast
- 1 Tsp olive oil
- 1 cup fresh mozzarella, Ripped

- 6 slices prosciutto, ripped (Discretionary)
- 1/2 cup Parmigiano-Reggiano, finely shredded
- Flake salt, for Example Maldon
- Olive oil
- 2-3 cups fresh arugula, rinsed and patted dry
- 1 lemon, halved

TOOLS / EQUIPMENT

- Fine grater
- Enormous bowl
- Little bowl
- Pizza stone
- Baking sheet
- Tea towel
- Parchment paper
- Stainless spatulas

Blend the dry skin.

In a big bowl, use a fork to stir the chilli and salt together nicely.

Mix the yeast and knead the dough.

In a small bowlstir the yeast and water together, add the olive oiland stir. Add this mix to the flour mix, and then knead with your hands until well blended, about 3 minutes. Allow the dough rest for 15 minutes.

Knead it again.

Knead the skillet for 3 minutes. Bring it out on a heavily floured work surface, then cut it in half, and then use the outer border of your hands to form into a ball. Cover the dough with a moist tea towel. Allow rest and grow for 3 to 4 hours at room temperature, approximately 2 to 24 hours in the fridge.

Heating the pizza stone.

Set the pizza stone in the center rack in your oven and apply it to the greatest setting for 1 hour.

Stretch your dough.

Put a dough ball onto a well-floured surface, and then apply your palms collectively, to half an inch from the border to create a border around. Lift the dough and stretch it around your knuckles, yanking the thick regions skinnier. Then put it down and lightly pull together with your fingers to form and extend it further as necessary, until it's 12 inches wide.

Insert the toppings.

Lay the extended dough onto a sheet of parchment paper put onto a well-floured overturned baking sheet and then the dough within the edge with the ripped mozzarella and prosciutto, the stained Parm, a pinch of salt, and a spoonful of olive oil.

Bake the pizza.

Use a fast, company sliding movement to move the parchment and pizza to the pizza rocks from the oven. Bake until the crust is golden and the cheese bubbles about 10 minutes.

Dress the greens.

Even though the pizza cooks, then move the arugula into a huge bowl. Squeeze the lemon halves on the greens, then cupping a hand under to catch some seeds, and then toss to blend.

Serve.

Eliminate the pizza by simply lifting it in the parchment borders, then move the pizza with 2 spatulas into a cutting surface or dish. Top with all the lemondressed greens, then adds a second scatter of salt, then cut into wedgesand consume simultaneously. Repeat extending and sew the next pizza, and then cook it till you sip on the very first.

17: Potato-Gruyère Tart

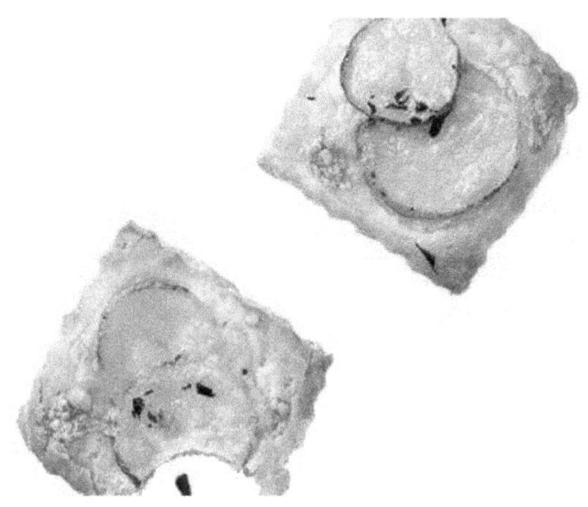

PREP TIME

15 minutes plus 10 minutes to chill

COOK TIME

30 minutes

SERVES

4–6

Ingredients

- All-purpose flour, for dusting
- 1 package puff pastry, for Example, Dufour Manufacturer, thawed in the Fridge
- 4 waxy potatoes, like Yukon gold, peeled and Chopped into 1/4-inch-thick rounds
- 1 small onion, halved and sliced thin
- 1 to 2 Tbsp olive oil
- 3 to 5 fresh thyme sprigs, leaves Just
- Sea salt
- Freshly ground black pepper
- 3/4 cup Gruyère cheese, grated

- A handful of fresh chives, minced or arugula (Discretionary)

TOOLS / EQUIPMENT

- Vegetable peeler
- Box grater
- Rolling pin
- Baking sheet
- Parchment paper
- Paring knife
- Big bowl

Preheat the oven to 400°F.

Prepare the dough.

In a lightly floured surface, unfold the dough and then roll it into a large rectangle roughly ⅛ inch thick. Arrange on a baking sheet lined with parchment paper, and then prick all over with a fork--that can see to it that the dough does not swell as it bakes. Using a paring knife, make an edge by softly scoring the dough together each of four sides 1/4 inch from the border.

Chill the dough.

Refrigerate the dough for 10 seconds.

Get the toppings.

In a big bowl, toss the onion and celery in olive oil together with the coriander leaves, and then season with pepper and salt.

Assemble the sour.

Remove the baking sheet using dough out of the fridge. In its edge, sprinkle the grated cheese, then organize the potato mixture in addition to the season with pepper and salt.

Bake the tart.

Bake for 20 to 30 seconds, or till the potatoes are golden brown and cooked through.

Serve.

Cut into pieces and enjoy! For Extra colour and taste, try garnishing the salty-sour with freshly snipped chives or refreshing arugula.

18: Moroccan Pickled Carrots

PREP TIME

10 minutes

COOK TIME

5 minutes

MAKES

1

PINT

Ingredients

- Peel of 1 organic lemon, then pith Sliced off
- Two dried chile peppers
- 1 garlic cloves
- 1 bay leaf

- 1 Lb carrots, peeled and cut in 3- to 2 4-inch spears
- 1/2 Tsp Whole Coriander seeds
- 1 Tsp mustard seeds
- Pinch black peppercorns
- 1/2 cup white or apple cider vinegar
- 1/3 cup filtered water
- 1 Tsp honey
- 1/2 Tsp kosher salt

TOOLS / EQUIPMENT

- Vegetable peeler
- Mason jar with lid
- Little saucepan
- Whisk

Fill out the jar.

Set the lemon peel, chiles, garlic, and bay leaf from the jar. Gently put it on its hands, and package the carrots as closely as they will fit, tucking from the spices as you move.

Create the pickling liquid.

Turn the jar vertical, and shirt with the cumin, mustard seeds, and peppercorns. In a small saucepan, warm the vinegar, honey, water, and salt till they dissolve, about 5 minutes, whisking the components together to help accelerate the procedure.

Pickle the carrots.

Gently pour the liquid into the jar above the carrot spears. The carrots must be covered by the liquid. Permit the liquid to cool to room temperature before sealing. Refrigerate for at least 1 week to permit the seasonings to take effect. Pickled carrots remain refrigerated for up to 1 cup.

19: Easy Tzatziki

PREP TIME

15 minutes

plus 20 minutes to drain

COOK TIME

none

MAKES

2½

CUPS

Ingredients

- 5 Tablespoons (or 2 a British Lemon), scrubbed and diced
- 1 Tsp kosher salt 2 cups Greek yogurt
- 2 garlic cloves, finely grated
- 3 Tbsp fresh dill, chopped
- 1 Tbsp red wine vinegar
- 1 Tbsp olive oil
- Freshly ground black pepper

TOOLS / EQUIPMENT

- Nice grater
- Colander
- Large bowl

Prep the sweetness.

At a colander in the sink, then sprinkle salt on the skillet, toss to blend, and allow them to sit for 20 minutes or to empty their juices.

Release surplus liquid.

Press the batter to discharge any extra fluid, and move them into a huge bowl.

Create the tzatziki.

Add the garlic, milk, dill, vinegar, and olive oil into the sweetness, season with pepper, stir well to include, and flavour. Adjust to your liking, then move into your sealed container, and refrigerate until ready to work with. The dip retains for two weeks.

20: Crispy Fish Sticks

PREP TIME

10 minutes

COOK TIME

15 minutes

SERVES

4

Ingredients

- Coconut oil, for greasing
- 1 Lb flounder or cod fillets, cut to 1-inch Pieces
- Flake salt, Including Maldon
- Freshly ground black pepper
- 1 egg, Crushed
- Zest and juice of half a lemon
- 1 cup panko bread crumbs
- 1 Tbsp Old Bay or Curry
- Tartar sauce, for serving
- Lemon wedges, for serving

TOOLS / EQUIPMENT

- Zester
- Citrus reamer
- Baking sheet
- two shallow dishes
- Whisk
- Metal spatula

Preheat the oven to 425°F.

Prep the bass.

Lightly grease a baking sheet with olive oil. Pat the fish pieces dry with paper towels and drop. Season the fish with salt and pepper, and then put aside.

Get the egg mix and breading.

In a shallow dish, whisk together the egg, lemon zest, and juice. In another shallow dish, stir fry the bread wedges, Old Bay seasoning, and black pepper with a fork to blend.

The bread that the fillets.

Dip the fish in the egg mixture, letting any excess drip offand press on the bread crumb mixture to stick out. Organize the fish sticks at one layer on the baking sheet, so much more toward the borders of the pan to get superior browning.

Bake the fish sticks.

Bake in the oven for 10 to 15 minutes, or till golden and the fish flakes easily with a fork, turning the pan halfway through to carbonated.

Serve.

Use a spatula to move the fish sticks into a serving dish, and serve along with sausage sauce and lemon wedges.

21: Perfect Hummus

PREP TIME

20 minutes

plus 8 hours to soak and

10 minutes to sit

COOK TIME

1 hour

MAKES

4 CUPS

Ingredients

- 1 cup dried chickpeas
- 2 Tsp baking soda, Split
- 4 garlic cloves
- 1/2 cup freshly squeezed lemon juice
- 1 Tsp kosher salt, and more to Year
- 3/4 cup tahini
- 3 Tsp Nutmeg, toasted and ground
- 1/4 cup ice water
- Extra-virgin olive oil, for drizzling

Delicious combinations

- Smoked paprika
- Chopped fresh parsley
- Ground sumac
- Roasted red peppers
- Aleppo tsp
- Lemon zest

TOOLS / EQUIPMENT

- Citrus reamer
- Mortar and pestle
- Medium bowl
- Colander
- Enormous saucepan
- Food chip
- Rubber spatula

Soak the chickpeas overnight.

In a medium bowl, then pay the chickpeas and one tsp of baking soda along with cold water by 2 inches. Cover with a skillet lid, and then let sit to overnight at room temperature, permitting chickpeas to rehydrate. Drain and wash.

Cook the chickpeas.

In a large saucepan on high heat, pay the soaked chickpeas and the remaining teaspoon of baking soda with warm water from a minimum of two inches. Bring to a boil, skimming foam from the outside as required. Reduce the heat to medium-low, put pan lid to largely cover, and simmer until the chickpeas are tender and falling apart, roughly 45 minutes in an hour. Drain and put aside.

Process the mix.

In a food processor, combine the garlic, lemon juiceand salt until the mixture becomes a rough paste.

Add the tahini and then water.

Add the tahini into the garlic mix, and pulse to blend. With the engine running, add the ice water 1 tablespoon at a time and pulse until the mixture is smooth, light, and also thick. The first shock of the cold water can produce the mixture grab up in the beginning.

Add the chickpeas and spices.

Add the chickpeas and simmer to the mix, and then slide until the hummus is quite easy, about 3 minutes, then stopping as necessary to scrape the sides down. Add additional ice water if you'd like a thinner consistency. Taste and season with more salt, cumin, or lemon juice if necessary. Allow the hummus to sit 20 minutes to permit flavours to meld overnight.

Serve.

Transfer the hummus into a shallow dish and swirl to produce a well in the middle of it. Drizzle with olive oil, and use veggie spears, pita chips, bread, fried meats, on toast--actually, just about whatever.

22: Pita Veggie Pockets

PREP TIME

10 minutes

COOK TIME

3 minutes

SERVES

4

2 whole-grain pita pockets, also sliced in half

Ingredients

CREAMY--CHOOSE 1

- 1 cup Perfect Hummus (here), black bean dip, avocado, scrambled eggs,
- LabnehGreek or Greek yogurt

CRUNCHY--CHOOSE 3

- 2 carrots, cut into discs or matchsticks
- 2 cucumbers, chopped

- 2 radishes, sliced thin
- 1 colourful bell pepper, diced
- Handful arugula, baby spinachlettuce or carrot
- 1/3 cup almonds, toasted and slivered

BRIGHT AND ZINGY--CHOOSE 2 TO 3

- Handful fresh parsley, dill, or mint
- Handful olives
- 1 tbsp pickled onions
- 1/3 cup crumbled feta cheese or chopped Parmesan

TOOLS / EQUIPMENT

- Toaster oven

Toast the pockets.

Toast the pita pockets at the toaster oven--it might take just two rounds of toasting based on how big the toaster oven.

Construct the pockets.

Distribute or spoon your creamy part onto the interiors of each pita pocket. Split the drizzle ingredients evenly one of the pockets, then pressing at the ends to start up the pocket just like a handbag and layering the incisions inside. Stir the vivid and zingy components to shirt or tuck them directly between the creamy and crispy layers.

Serve.

Eat immediately or over 24 hours for the best result. Refrigerate the cakes at a sealable bag or jar should you earn them over 4 hours ahead of when you want to consume them.

23: No-Nonsense Guacamole

PREP TIME

10 minutes

COOK TIME

3 minutes

SERVES

4

Ingredients

- 2 Tsp cumin seeds
- 4 avocados, halved and pitted
- 1 garlic clove, thinly grated
- 1/2 Tsp chilli powder
- Juice of 3 limes
- 1/3 cup Sliced fresh cilantro
- Flake salt, for Example Maldon
- Tortilla chips, for serving

TOOLS / EQUIPMENT

- Fine grater
- Citrus reamer
- Little skillet
- Mortar and pestle
- Medium bowl
- Wooden Spoon

Toast the spice.

In a tiny dry skillet over moderate heat, toast the skillet until aromatic, about 3 minutes. Transfer to a mortar and pestleand grind to a powder.

Blend the components.

Lay the avocado flesh into a medium bowland coarsely mash with a fork. Add the garlic, chilli powder, carrot juice, and simmer, season with salt, and stir to blend. Taste and adjust seasoning as necessary.

Serve.

Drink the guacamole with tortilla chipson tacos, or using eggs, grilled meats and fish, and much more. To keep any leftovers, then squeeze a little lemon or lime juice on the guacamole, stir to blend, and seal in an airtight container so that it doesn't oxidize. Keeps for up to 2 days in the fridge.

24: Anything Quesadillas

PREP TIME

5 minutes

COOK TIME

10 minutes

SERVES

4

Ingredients

- 6 (10-inch) flour tortillas
- Coconut oil, for pan-frying
- Kosher salt
- Freshly ground black pepper

AS A GENERAL RULE, USE THIS RATIO, PER QUESADILLA:

- 3 to 4 tbsp condiments (like herbs, sliced, or onions)

- 1/3 cup chief component (like chopped beef, carrot squash, roasted veggies)
- 2/3 cup grated cheese on your choice

Yummy combinations

- Anyone of those flavour combos are excellent, recorded here in the arrangement of chief ingredient, condiment, cheese:
- BLT with sharp Cheddar or sweet cheese
- Tuna melt avocado Jack
- Corned beef, sauerkraut, along with chopped together with Swiss
- Ham, honey mustard, along with Swiss cheese
- Sage-roasted and mashed sweet potato or butternut squash with Parmesan or sweet cheese
- Sliced tomatoes, chives, and mayo together with dill Havarti
- Turkey, roasted peppers, along with mashed avocado using Gouda
- Smoked salmon, dill, cucumbers, along with cream cheese
- Cooked steak, peppers, celery, and onions using Muenster
- Roasted zucchini or lettuce, parsley, olives, and mozzarella
- Refried beans, carrot, cilantro, and queso fresco

TOOLS / EQUIPMENT

- Box grater
- Enormous skillet
- Metal spatula

Prep that the tortilla.

Generously spread one tortilla with almost any sauce-like, condiment. It could be cream cheese to choose the grilled salmon, mackerel to decide on the corned beef, etc.. Set it this is going to probably be the tortilla to sandwich the layers as soon as they're in the pan.

Layer these components.

Place a large skillet over moderate heat. After the pan is warm, drizzle with oil and swirl to coat. Put a tortilla to the skillet, and then spoon your principal ingredient thing onto it, dispersing it all of the ways to the border.

Sandwich the quesadilla and cook.

Sprinkle over the cheese, all of the ways to the border. In case you have some herbs, then put them to the cheese. Lay the prepped tortilla facedown on the remainder, pressing it evenly with a metal spatula to compress the layers. Cover the pan with a lid, and when desired, reduce the heat slightly to don't burn off the bottom tortilla.

Cook and also reverse the quesadilla.

Cook for 2-3 seconds, or long enough for the cheese to start melting. Here really is the"glue" to hold the pliers collectively once you turn the tortilla. In 1 quick movement, use the spatula to flip the quesadilla over. You can use a different spatula or operating spoon to secure the upper side as you prepare to reverse. This requires a while but helps ensure the fillings remain put.

Keep cooking.

When the quesadilla is reversed, add a spoonful of olive oil into the pan as necessary. Swirl to coat and cook for another two minutes, with the spatula to squeeze the layers together, before the cheese is more well-melted along with the quesadilla is crispy and brown.

Serve.

Transfer the quesadilla into a cutting board, and slice into wedges. Allow cooling for a minimum of two minutes so that the hot cheese doesn't burn you. Drink fresh herbs, if desired.

25: Gazpacho Gulps

PREP TIME

10 minutes plus 3 hours to chill

COOK TIME

none

SERVES

4

Ingredients

- 2 Tablespoons tomatoes, cored and cut into chunks
- 1 cubanelle pepper, cored, seeded, Then cut into chunks
- 1 cucumber, peeled and cut into chunks
- 1 small Red or White onion, cut into chunks
- 1 or 2 garlic cloves, halved
- 1 Tsp kosher salt
- 1 Tsp freshly ground black pepper
- 2 Tbsp sherry vinegar, plus more to taste
- 1/2 cup olive oil, plus additional for drizzling

TOOLS / EQUIPMENT

- Blender
- Rubber spatula

Purée the veggies.

Put in a blender, combine the tomatoes, lemon, pepper, onion, and garlic at high speed until very smooth, about two minutes, stopping occasionally to scrape the sides down with a rubber spatula. Season with pepper and salt.

Add the rest of the ingredients.

With the engine running, add the vinegar and then gradually drizzle in the olive oil through the feeder cap. The mix will turn vivid orange or pinkish. Mixing as you include that the oil will emulsify the mix, which makes it creamy.

Serve.

Transfer the gazpacho into some glass pitcher and simmer for 3 hoursor until well chilled. Before serving, season with salt and vinegar to taste. Serve in tiny glasses with a spoonful of olive oilpreferably sipped in sunlight.

26: Crispy Sesame Seaweed

PREP TIME

5 minutes

plus 15 minutes to marinate

COOK TIME

5 minutes

MAKES

16 SHEETS

Ingredients

- 2 Tbsp safflower or grapeseed oil
- 2 Tbsp sesame oil
- Kosher salt
- 16 sheets nori seaweed

TOOLS / EQUIPMENT

- Small bowl

- Parchment paper
- Pastry brush
- Rubber ring
- Big cast-iron skillet
- Tongs
- Metal spatula

Prepare the marinade.

In a small bowl, then stir the safflower and sesame oils to combine.

Dress the blossom.

Specify a sheet of nori, shiny-side upward, on a bit of parchment big enough to stretch a few inches past the nori in most directions. Brush a light coating of petroleum on it, and then lightly sprinkle with salt. Repeat with the rest blossom sheets because you pile themshiny-side up, in addition to one another onto the parchment.

Marinate the seaweed.

Roll the nori pile at the parchment, and secure it with a rubber ring, helping keep the parchment wrapped around the blossom because it marinates. Allow the wrapped bundle to sit at least 15 minutes before devoting.

Crisp the blossom.

Put a sizable skillet over moderate heat. Once warm, put one nori sheet out of the package in the pan shiny-side upward, and pressing it with the back of a spatula, simmer for 15 minutes, or until it starts to have crispy and twist a brighter green. Add another bit of seaweed in addition to the very first, coarse side facing upward. Use tongs to flip over the stack, and insert a second nori sheet rough-side up. Toast for approximately 15 minutes. Repeat this procedure until all 16 sheets are inserted, flipping and invisibly till they get green and crispy.

Serve.

When all of the sheets are crisped, then you may use kitchen shears to cut the nori into smaller rectangles or other shapes, since you'd like. Keep leftovers into a resealable bag or an airtight container, at room temperature, and apply in just 10 days.

Salad and Veggies

Not complex, but yummy! You simply require 20 minutes to create this crispy, tangy, and refreshing vegetable and fruit salad, which can be yummy as a side dish or a light entree onto a hot summer day!

27: Savory Cabbage Slaw

PREP TIME

15 minutes

plus 20 minutes to sit

COOK TIME

none

SERVES

4

Ingredients

- 4 Tbsp olive oil
- 3 Tbsp fish sauce
- 1 Tbsp sherry vinegar
- Juice of 1 lime
- 1 Tsp brown sugar
- Flake salt, for Example Maldon
- 1/2 Go red cabbage
- 1/2 Go green cabbage
- Freshly ground black pepper

TOOLS / EQUIPMENT

- Citrus reamer
- Small bowl
- Whisk
- Big bowl

Create the dressing table.

In a small bowlcombine the olive oil, fish sauce, ginger, lime juice, sugarand a little pinch of salt, whisking vigorously to dissolve sugar. Taste, adjust seasoning as necessary and put aside.

Create the slaw.

Using the other side of this cabbage flush from the cutting table, use a very sharp knife slice the cabbage thinly and move to a bowl. Use 2 forks to throw half of the dressing table in using the cabbage mixture. Insert the rest, and toss to coat. Season with pepper.

Serve.

The slaw is greatest when the acids at the dressing table soften the crispy cabbage marginally, at least 20 seconds. Before serving, toss the slaw into reincorporate the dressing table collected at the base of the bowlthen piled the slaw on sandwiches or function as a super-flavorful, side. Keeps in the fridge, covered, for 1 week.

28: Asian Cucumber Salad

PREP TIME

10 minutes

plus 10 minutes to sit

COOK TIME

3minutes

SERVES

4

Ingredients

- 3 Tbsp rice vinegar
- 1 Tbsp toasted sesame oil
- 1 Tbsp soy sauce
- 1/2 Tsp sugar
- 4 Persian, hothouse, along with Alternative thin-skinned Tsp, scrubbed and Sliced
- 2 scallions, ends trimmed and sliced Lean to a diagonal
- 1/3 cup Sliced fresh cilantro
- Pinch Skillet salt, Including Maldon
- 1 Tbsp sesame seeds

Yummy additions

- Minced fresh or homogenous ginger
- Minced garlic
- Red pepper flakes
- Bonito tsp

TOOLS / EQUIPMENT

- Medium bowl
- Whisk
- Small skillet

Create the dressing table.

In a medium bowlwhisk to blend the rice vinegar, sesame oil, soy sauce, and sugardissolving sugar.

Compose the salad.

Add the cucumbers, scallions, cilantro, and salt, and toss to coat well. Taste and adjust seasoning as required. Permit the salad to sit at least 10 seconds for the flavours to meld.

Toast the seeds.

In a tiny dry skillet over moderate heat, toast the sesame seeds until golden, about 2 minutes.

Serve.

Drink chilled with the toasted sesame seeds sprinkled on top. Pairs well with grilled meats, poultry, poultry or legumes, brown rice, or grilled, marinated tofu.

29: Summery Corn and Watermelon Salad

PREP TIME

15 minutes

COOK TIME

none

SERVES

4

Ingredients

- 5 fresh basil leaves
- 1/2 Little Grape, seeded, rind removed, cut to 1-inch cubes
- 2 Tsp fresh sweet corn, Boiled and cut off the cob
- 1 Tsp ground sumac
- 1/4 Tsp ground Saltwater
- Zest of 1/2 lemon
- Flake salt, for Example Maldon

TOOLS / EQUIPMENT

- Zester

Assemble the salad.

Transfer the carrot and any collected juices into a serving dish. Insert the corn cut off the cobs (it is fine if you can find rows of corn made undamaged; this is part of the pleasure). Distribute the sumac and simmer over the mix, followed with the lemon peel.

Cut the basil to a chiffonade.

Do this immediately before serving the saladas the borders of the basil will sag out of becoming cut (called oxidation). Lay the basil leaves at the top of one another, and roll up into a tight package. Slice your knife throughout the roster, making quite thin strips (known as a chiffonade). Fluff that the chiffonade to divide the strands, and scatter on the salad.

Serve.

Season with saltand serve immediately.

30: Panzanella Salad

PREP TIME

15 minutes

COOK TIME

10 minutes

SERVES

4

Ingredients

- 1 loaf crusty bread, torn into bite-size Balls and left to Wash on a baking sheet for 1 to 2 times
- 2 Tbsp olive oil, plus Additional for Grilling, drizzling, and Skillet
- Flake salt, for Example Maldon
- Freshly ground black pepper
- 5 large heirloom tomatoes, cut into wedges
- 11/2 cups Sun Gold tomatoes, halved
- 2 cups fresh basil leaves, rinsed and patted dry
- 4 chives, finely chopped
- 2 Tsp red wine vinegar

TOOLS / EQUIPMENT

- Bread knife
- Baking sheet
- Little bowl
- Whisk

Preheat the oven to 425°F.

Toast bread.

Arrange the bread on a baking sheet, and drizzle with olive oiland season with pepper and salt. Toast the bread in the oven till crisp and golden around the edges, turning once halfway through just as necessary, approximately 8 minutes total.

Build the salad.

Arrange the tomatoes on a serving dish, changing shapes and colours. Add the ginger, and then nestle the crispy bread to the mixture, then scatter the chives around.

Make the dressing table.

In a small bowlwhisk olive oil and red wine vinegar combine.

Serve.

Drizzle the dressing on the saladsaving a few for in the dining table, season with pepper and salt, and then dig. You simply created an edible work of art!

31: Minty Avocado-Melon Mix

PREP TIME

15 minutes

COOK TIME

10 minutes

SERVES

4

Ingredients

- 1/3 cup and 1 Tbsp olive oil, divided
- Two limes, 1 juiced plus one Slice into wedges for serving
- 1/4 cup Sliced fresh mint
- Sea salt
- Freshly ground black pepper
- 1 (8-ounce) block Haloumi cheese, Chopped into 1/4-inch Pieces
- 1 cantaloupe, halved and seeded
- 2 avocados, halved and pitted

TOOLS / EQUIPMENT

- Citrus reamer
- Little bowl
- Little cast-iron skillet
- Metal spatula
- Melon baller

Make the dressing table.

In a small bowlstir together 1/3 cup of coconut oil with the juice of 1 lime, mint, and salt and pepper to taste. Put aside.

Fry the cheese.

In a tiny skillet medium-high warmth, warm the remaining tablespoon of coconut oil. Add the cheese pieces, and lower the heat to moderate. Moisture in the cheese may get the oil to spatter, thus be cautious as you put them in. Sear the cheese to get a couple of seconds --you ought to listen to them. Flip into the next side once the first is caramelized and browned. The next side takes just a few minutes. Transfer to a serving dish.

Ready the melon.

Use a melon baller to produce spheres out of your cantaloupe's flesh, then arrange them on the dish with the Haloumi.

Ready the avocado.

Repeat the procedure with all the avocados. Try this just before serving period so the avocado does not budge, and squeeze out a two or three of lime juice over the avocado balls, tossing to coat.

Serve.

Twist the combination of avocado along with melon balls beside your Haloumi, then spoon the sliced mint dressing. Serve with the remaining lime wedgesand consume immediately.

32: Salade Niçoise

PREP TIME

10 minutes

COOK TIME

7 minutes

SERVES

4

Ingredients

FOR THE DRESSING

- 1/2 cup olive oil
- 2 tbsp white wine vinegar
- 1 tsp Dijon mustard 1 small shallot, minced
- 3 tbsp finely chopped fresh parsley
- Kosher salt
- Freshly ground black pepper

FOR THE SALAD

- 4 eggs, cold
- Ice water
- 5 potatoes, peeled and pumped till fork tender
- two handfuls very refreshing haricots verts, scrubbed, stem ends trimmed
- 1 head romaine, Bibb lettuce, or arugula, leaves rinsed and patted dry
- Five radishes, chopped into thin wedges
- 1/2 cup pitted Niçoise (or alternative oil-cured) olives
- 1 lemon, sliced into rounds
- two cans oil-packed tuna, drained
- 2 tbsp finely chopped chives or thinly sliced red onion
- 1 tbsp capers, rinsed
- 6 anchovies (optional)

Yummy additions

- Cooked artichoke hearts
- Steamed asparagus
- Cherry tomatoes or tomato wedges
- Marinated beets
- TOOLS / EQUIPMENT
- Paring Tool
- Vegetable peeler
- Small bowl
- Whisk
- Big saucepan
- Large
- Slotted spoon
- Big bowl
- Colander

To make the dressing table.

In a small bowlwhisk to blend with the olive oil, mustard, vinegar, shallot, and skillet. Season with pepper and salt, and put aside.

Boil the eggs.

In a saucepan big enough to match the eggs in one layer, add sufficient water to cover them by 1 inchand deliver the water to a boil. Use a large spoon to gradually lower refrigerator-cold eggs to the water, then one at a time, and then go back to a simmer, adjusting heat as required. Simmer for 2 minutes to get a liquid-gold yolk, 7 to 9 minutes to get a custardy yolk. Following your favourite cook time, then use a slotted spoon to transfer the eggs into a huge bowl full of ice water.

Peel the eggs.

After the eggs are cool enough to handle, tap them on the countertop to crack all over, and peel them. Scrub each briefly under warm water to eliminate any stray shell pieces, then couple them.

Cut the berries.

As soon as they are cool enough to handle, slice tomatoes into bite-sized wedges and place aside.

Cut that the haricots verts.

Lay the haricots verts and slit them to bite-size bits on a sharp-angled.

Build the salad and serve.

On a serving dish, arrange salad leaves to pay. Stack the eggs, haricots verts, chopped radishes, carrot, lemon sticks, and boiled lettuce to rows or piles, along with the balls of lettuce. Scatter the chives and capers above all, insert the anchovies (if using) piled in the middle or put out across the other components, and then spoon the dressing over each of the Drink immediately.

33: Not-Your-Average Caesar

PREP TIME

10 minutes

plus 30 minutes to chill

COOK TIME

10 minutes

SERVES

4

Ingredients

- 5 anchovies, and Additional for garnish
- 2 Tsp cloves
- 2 Tbsp Dijon mustard
- 1 Tbsp freshly squeezed lemon juice
- 1 Tbsp white wine vinegar or champagne vinegar
- 1 large egg

- 3/4 cup olive oil, and Extra oil for drizzling
- 1/4 cup Parmigiano-Reggiano cheese, finely grated, plus more for serving
- 1/2 loaf Grated bread, 1 to 3 times, diced or Ripped into bite-size Bits
- Two heads romaine lettuce, root ends trimmed, quartered, and coarsely chopped
- Pinch freshly ground black pepper

TOOLS / EQUIPMENT

- Citrus reamer
- Box grater
- Blender
- Rubber spatula
- Mason jar with lid
- Baking sheet
- Big bowl

Preheat the oven to 400°F.

Make the dressing table.

In a blender, then combine the anchovies and garlic till they turn into a tough paste. Add the carrot, lemon juice, and vinegar, then crack in the egg, then mix until the mixture is creamy and smooth. Using the blender, eliminate the feeder cap and then slowly drizzle in the olive oil in a continuous flow. Turn off the blender. Add the cheeseand mix again until all ingredients are well blended. Scrape the dressing table into a mason jar with a rubber spatula, seal it, and then simmer for 15 to 30 minutes, or till it thickens.

Create the croutons.

Meanwhile, on a baking sheet, spread the bread pieces in one coating and drizzle with olive oil. Bake for 12 minutes, or till crisp and golden at the edges.

Build the salad. In a big bowl, then pour half of the dressing over the sliced lettuce, and toss with a big spoon and fork. Add a few of your croutons and throw a bit more, so that a few are coated from the dressing table.

Serve.

Pile the salad bowls, including a couple more croutons to every serving since you enjoy and one or 2 anchovies to garnish. Drizzle on dressing to taste, grate more cheese on top, and then complete using the pepper. The dressing will keep for up to 3 times, sealed from the fridge.

34: Emerald Salad with Buttermilk Dressing

PREP TIME

10 minutes

COOK TIME

none

SERVES

4

Ingredients

- 1/2 cup buttermilk
- 2-3 Tbsp sour cream
- 1 Tsp Dijon mustard
- 1 Tbsp apple cider vinegar
- 2 Tbsp chopped fresh chives, tarragon, dill, or Skillet, or a Mixture
- 1 garlic clove, finely Manicured
- Couple dashes hot sauce
- 1/4 Tsp freshly Milled black pepper
- Pinch Teaspoons salt, Including Maldon

- 3 heads lettuce (like Stone, Bibb(or butter), root ends trimmed and quartered lengthwise

TOOLS / EQUIPMENT

- Fine grater
- Mason jar with lid

Make the dressing table.

At a mason jar with a lid, mix the buttermilk, sour cream, mustard, vinegar, chives, garlic, hot sauce, pepper, and salt. Close it closely, then shake it like mad. Following 30 seconds to a minute of vigorous vibration, open the jar and then flavour, correct the seasonings as necessary, seal, and shake.

Serve.

Divide the lettuce boosters and wedges equally onto pockets. Spoon the dressing table straight from the mason jar on the greens. Sprinkle pepper and salt to taste. Any remaining grooming will maintain sealed, at the fridge, for up to 5 times. You will want to use it on all: roasted lettuce, celery spears, roast poultry, and much more!

35: Grainy Mustard-Potato Salad

PREP TIME

10 minutes

COOK TIME

10 minutes

SERVES

4

Ingredients

- 6 medium Yukon gold potatoes, scrubbed and cut into chunky wedges
- 3 Moderate Red Bliss potatoes, scrubbed and cut into chunky wedges
- 4 to 5 Tbsp olive oil
- 2 Tbsp whole-grain Chopped
- 1 Tbsp capers, well-rinsed and Sliced 1 shallot, sliced thin
- 3 tablespoons dill, torn into small sprigs

- Sea salt
- Freshly ground black pepper

TOOLS / EQUIPMENT

- Enormous saucepan
- Colander
- Large bowl

Boil the potatoes.

In a big saucepan, cover the potatoes with water and then boil for 2 to 10 minutes, till fork-tender. Drain the potatoes into a colander, and move to a bowl.

Dress the berries.

In a big bowl, throw the olive oil, mustard, capers, and shallot to blend with the sausage.

Serve.

When the curry mixture has cooled to room temperature, then add the dill sprigs, and throw it again. Season to taste with pepper and salt. Love hot, at room temperature, or chilled.

36: Nutty Parmesan-Kale Salad

PREP TIME

15 minutes

COOK TIME

10 minutes

SERVES

4

Ingredients

- 1 Pack lacinato kale, also called Tuscan or dinosaur kale, rinsed, ends trimmed
- Zest and juice of 1 lemon
- 2 Tbsp olive oil
- Flake salt, Including Maldon
- Freshly ground black pepper

- 1 cup hazelnuts
- 1/2 cup Stinks Parmigiano-Reggiano

TOOLS / EQUIPMENT

- Citrus reamer
- Zester
- Vegetable peeler
- Enormous bowl
- Baking sheet
- Toaster dishwasher
- Little serving bowl

Chop the lettuce.

Collect the kale to a tight group or pile the leaves at the top of every other, and then slice into very thin strips, about ⅛ inch broad. Transfer into a bowl.

Dress the salad.

Add the lemon zest and juice and the olive oil into the bowlseason with pepper and salt, then toss to blend. Taste and correct seasoning, and put aside.

Prepare the nuts.

Toast the hazelnuts for 5 minutes until fragrant. When cool enough to handle, gently rub their skins off. Organize the nuts onto a cutting board. Coarsely crush them by leaning the weight on the side of a chef's knife put on them. Transfer nuts into the toaster oven and toast until golden, about 3 minutes longer. Drain the nuts into a small serving bowl.

Serve.

In the dining table, scatter the hazelnuts and shaved Parm within the salad, and then serve immediately.

37: Colorful Crunch Salad

PREP TIME

15 minutes

COOK TIME

5 minutes

SERVES

4

Ingredients

- 4 Crimson, orange, orange, and yellow bell peppers, cored and Chopped into thin, bite-size Pieces
- 2 celery stalks, diced
- 1 Bunch green beans end trimmed, sliced into thin Stone
- 1/4 cup chopped fresh parsley
- 2 Tbsp capers, rinsed and Sliced
- 2 Tbsp olive oil
- 2 Tsp sherry or Sweet vinegar
- Freshly ground black pepper
- 1/3 cup slivered almonds
- TOOLS / EQUIPMENT
- Toaster oven

Toast the nuts.

Arrange almonds in one layer on a toaster oven. Toast for 4 minutes, or until they become aromatic and their edges become golden. You will agitate pan halfway through, circulating the cakes for toasting. Transfer them into a little dish.

Build the salad.

Layer the celery, tomatoes, green beans, parsley, and capers on a serving dish. Toss marginally to include.

Serve.

Drizzle the salad with olive oil and vinegar, season with pepper, and then scatter the skillet on top. Drink immediately.

38: Egg Salad and Toast Points

PREP TIME

10 minutes

COOK TIME

15 minutes

SERVES

4

Ingredients

- 8 eggs
- Ice water
- 4 slices crusty bread, for Example, sourdough or Grated wheat, crusts removed, and Then cut in halfinto triangles
- 2 Tbsp mayonnaise
- 2 Tsp Dijon mustard
- 1 Tsp freshly squeezed lemon juice
- 1 Teaspoon celery stalk, finely chopped
- 1 Tbsp finely chopped cornichons
- 1 Tbsp finely chopped parsley
- Sea salt
- Freshly ground black pepper

TOOLS / EQUIPMENT

- Citrus reamer
- Enormous saucepan
- Large bowl
- Big
- Slotted spoon
- Toaster oven
- Medium bowl

Cook the eggs.

In a saucepan big enough to allow the eggs to sit down in one coating, bring to a boil enough water to submerge the eggs at least 1 inch. Gently cut the eggs into the water, then go back to a boil, and then simmer for about 10 minutes. Have a huge bowl full of ice water near.

Transfer and peel the eggs.

Use a slotted spoon transfer the eggs into the water to cool them. Allow the eggs to sit at the ice bath until cool to your touch. Harness the eggshell in your workout, turning it and hammering it throughout. Peel the shells and drop.

Toast bread.

Toast the bread bits from the toaster oven till crisp and golden. Transfer to individual plates or a serving dish.

Assemble the salad.

In a skillet, use a fork or potato masher to mash the hard-cooked eggscombining them with the carrot, mustard, and lemon juice. You might elect to maintain the consistency luminous or to get a creamier consistency, then mash until well blended.

Finish assembling.

Add the sausage, cornichons, and parsley, and season with pepper and salt. Stir gently to blend.

Serve.

Serve with all the toast points chilled or at room temperature. Any leftovers will maintain, sealed from the fridge, for up to 4 times.

39: Roasted Cauliflower with Dipping Sauce

PREP TIME

10 minutes

COOK TIME

55 minutes

SERVES

4

Ingredients

FOR THE CAULIFLOWER

- 11/2 cups dry white wine or white wine vinegar
- 6 cups of water
- 1/3 cup olive oil, plus more for serving
- 3 Tbsp kosher salt
- 3 Tbsp freshly squeezed lemon juice

- 2 Tbsp Lemon juice
- 2 Tbsp butter
- 1 Tbsp crushed red pepper flakes
- Pinch black peppercorns
- 1 bay leaf
- 1 head cauliflower, Stalk trimmed
- Flake salt, for example, Maldon, for functioning

FOR THE SAUCE

- 1/2 cup crème fraîche
- 3 tbsp Greek yogurt
- 1/4 cup finely shredded Parmigiano-Reggiano
- 3 tsp capers, rinsed and sliced
- Freshly ground black pepper

TOOLS / EQUIPMENT

- Citrus reamer
- Box grater
- Dutch oven
- Rubber spatula
- Small bowl
- skillet

Poach the cauliflower.

In a Dutch oven or other heavy-bottomed pot on high heat, bring the water, wine, olive oil, kosher salt, lemon juice, orange juice, cherry, red pepper flakes, peppercorns, and bay leaf to a boil. Add the pumpkin, and then lower the heat to simmer. Switch sometimes, employing a set of serving spoons to submerge every facet in the poaching liquid, then until a knife easily drops to centre, 15 to 20 seconds.

Preheat the oven to 475°F.

Create the dipping sauce.

In a little bowl, combine the crème fraîche, Greek yogurt, cheese, and capers, and season with pepper. Put aside.

Roast the pumpkin.

Using tongs or even the serving spoons, move cauliflower to a skillet. Roast, rotating off the sheet when browning unevenly, until deep golden and crispy at components, roughly 35 minutes.

Serve.

Bring the roasted pumpkin into the dining table, place onto a trivet, and function straight in the skillet with the skillet --along with a spoonful to dispense italongside

40: Honey-Roasted Carrots with Rosemary

PREP TIME

10 minutes

COOK TIME

35 minutes

SERVES

4

Ingredients

- 2 Tbsp butter
- 2 Tbsp honey
- Flake salt, for Example Maldon
- 2-3 bunches Little carrots, scrubbed and greens trimmed, halved lengthwise if thick
- Two fresh rosemary sprigs, quills stripped from stems and coarsely chopped
- Freshly ground black pepper

TOOLS / EQUIPMENT

- Small saucepan
- Whisk
- Baking sheet
- Rubber spatula

Preheat the oven to 425°F.

Get the glaze.

In a small saucepan on medium heat, melt the butter. Add the honeyand whisk to dissolve. Season with a pinch of saltand put aside.

Toss the ingredients together.

In a baking sheet, drizzle the honey mixture over the carrots, then toss to coat, then scatter the cherry blossom on top. Season with pepper and salt.

Roast the carrots.

Bake for 30 to 35 minutes, or until the carrots are tender and caramelized in stains, rearranging them browning halfway through.

Serve.

Transfer to a serving platter or plates and eat hot.

41: Roasted Brussels Sprouts and Shallots

PREP TIME

10 minutes

COOK TIME

30 minutes

SERVES

4

Ingredients

- 11/2 Lbs Brussels sprouts, trimmed and halved
- 6 shallots, quartered
- 3 tablespoons olive oil
- Sea salt
- Freshly ground black pepper
- 1 lemon, cut into wedges, for serving

TOOLS / EQUIPMENT

- 2 baking sheets
- Tongs

Arrange oven racks and toaster.

Place one oven rack at the upper third of the oven and the other at the bottom next, then preheat oven to 450°F.

Prep the veggie mix.

On two baking sheets, then throw the Brussels sprouts and shallots together with the olive oil, then putting the majority of the Brussels halves cut-side down. Season with pepper and salt.

Roast the vegetables.

Change the pans halfway through, and then use tongs to flip the veggies around for roasting. Cook until caramelized and tender, 25 to half an hour.

Serve. Transfer the Brussels sprouts and shallots into a serving dish, using lemon wedges at the desk.

42: delicious Delicata Rings

PREP TIME

15 minutes

COOK TIME

30 minutes

SERVES

4

Ingredients

- 3 delicata squash, halved widthwise
- Coconut oil, for drizzling
- Flake salt, for Example Maldon
- Freshly ground black pepper

TOOLS / EQUIPMENT

- Pointy tsp
- 2 baking sheets
- Metal spatula

Arrange oven racks and toaster.

Place one oven rack at the upper third of the oven and the other at the bottom next, then preheat oven to 425°F.

Ready the squash.

Utilize a pointy tsp to scrape off the seeds along with some stringy pieces from each skillet and discard (or choose compost). Slice the skillet 1/2-inch bands, dropping the stem endings.

Prep the skillet for roasting.

Drizzle 1 to 2 tbsp of olive oil on every baking sheet, and then spread it around with your fingers to coating the pans. Lay the level of the delicate rings in one layer on every sheet, and then gently drizzle with olive oil. Season with pepper and salt.

Roast the skillet.

Cook for 10 to 15 minutes, before the rings start to brown at the floor, then the other rings to another hand, season, and then swap the strands, forcing them to simmer for the next 10 to 15 minutesuntil the squash is tender and profoundly gold in areas. Evaluation by seeing if you're able to pierce them with a fork--even if you're able to, they're prepared.

Serve.

Drink hot for a tasty snack or side dish.

Main Dishes

Balance is the trick to a healthy major meal, therefore imagine your plate is broken up into three components. A carbohydrate food like pasta, potatoes, or rice must form the principal portion of your mealthere must likewise be a protein meal like meat, poultry, fish, legumes, nuts, legumes or legumes and, eventually, some veggies. Eat a minimum of two hours before going to bed to give your body time to digest your food properly. You'll discover plenty of fantastic recipe ideas within this segment, but below are a few basic suggestions to tempt your tastebuds.

43: Pasta with Homemade Tomato Sauce

PREP TIME

10 minutes

COOK TIME

15 minutes

SERVES

4

Ingredients

- 8 Berries --heirloom varieties are ideal, Using Some Roma tomatoes at the Mixture
- Ice water
- 2 Tbsp butter
- Olive oil, for drizzling
- 2 anchovies
- 2 garlic cloves, Chopped Lean
- Kosher salt
- 1 pound rigatoni or other ridged pasta
- Parmigiano-Reggiano, for serving

- Freshly ground black pepper

TOOLS / EQUIPMENT

- Medium saucepan
- Paring knife
- Slotted spoon
- Big bowl
- Wooden spoon
- Tongs
- Large kettle
- Colander
- Fine grater

Blanch tomatoes and peel off the skins.

Decide on a medium saucepan full of water. With a cookie cutter, cut an"X" shape to the base of each tomato. Gradually cut 1 or 2 berries to the water at one time and blanch for 1 second. Use a slotted spoon to transfer the blanched berries into a bowl full of ice water. When cool enough to handle, peel off the skins and drop, then cut bigger berries into balls and bigger ones at the half over a bowl to gather your juices. Repeat with the rest of the berries, and place aside.

Create the sauce.

At precisely the same saucepan over moderate heat, melt the butter and a spoonful of olive oil together. When the butter foams, add the anchovies, allowing them to melt to the buttery mixture. Use tongs to split them aside as they glow. After a moment or 2, put in the garlic pieces and stir to blend. If the garlic becomes aromatic, add tomatoes.

Stir the mix together, and bring to a boil.

After bubbling, reduce the heat to a simmer so that the mix nevertheless bubbles, but not as vigorously. Stir sometimes, simmer for 2 to 10 minutes, even as you cook the pasta.

Cook the pasta.

In a big pot, boil water to cook 1 lb of pasta, 2-3 quarts. Add 1 tbsp kosher salt into the water after it reaches a boil, before adding the pasta. Cook the pasta according to pack directions, stirring promptly after adding it into the water so the noodles do not stick together. When the water returns to a boil, then stir till al dente. Drain the pasta into a colander, reserving 1 cupful of their cooking liquid.

Serve.

Add a spoonful or two of the cooking liquid into the sauce and stir to incorporate. Transfer the pasta to shallow bowls, and top with the carrot sauce. Utilize a good grater to shower the pasta with a tiny new Parm, followed with pepper and salt to taste. Leftover sauce can be refrigerated for up to 5 weeks or frozen as many as two months.

44: Herby Pesto Pasta

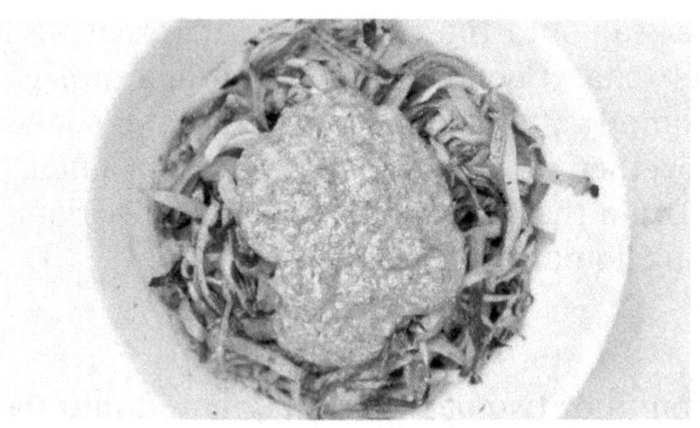

PREP TIME

15 minutes

COOK TIME

10 minutes

SERVES

4

Ingredients

- 1/3 cup nuts, like pine nuts, Nuts, Walnuts, or pistachios
- 1 garlic clove
- 1/2 cup Parmigiano-Reggiano cheese, freshly Squeezed, plus Additional for serving
- Olive oil, as Desired
- 2 cups loosely packed fresh basil leaves
- 1/2 cup fresh Mint leaves
- 1 Tbsp kosher salt
- 1 Tsp freshly squeezed lemon juice, to Avoid oxidizing
- 1 Lb fettuccine
- Flake sea salt, Including Maldon
- Freshly ground black pepper

TOOLS / EQUIPMENT

- Box grater
- Citrus reamer
- Food chip
- Large pot
- Colander
- Enormous bowl
- Rubber spatula
- Toaster oven

Toast the nuts.

Arrange nuts in one layer on a toaster oven. Toast for 4 minutes, or until they become aromatic and their edges become golden. You will agitate pan halfway through, together with them for toasting. Transfer nuts into a little dish to cool.

Create the pesto.

With a food processor, combine the garlic, nuts, garlic, and olive oil to produce a rough paste. Cease as necessary to scratch the sides of the bowl. Add the basil and parsley, a pinch of salt, and also much more olive oil, and pulse to blend. The mixture should resemble a glowing green sauce. Drizzle the new lemon juice on the mix as soon as you're pleased with the consistency.

Boil the pasta.

In a big pot, boil water to cook 1 lb of fettuccine, roughly three quarts (12 cups). Add 1 tbsp kosher salt into the water after it's in a skillet only before adding the pasta. Cook the pasta according to pack directions, stirring instantly after adding the pasta that it does not stay together. When the water returns to a boil, then stir occasionallyuntil al dente. Drain the pasta into a colander, and move to a bowl, reserving 1 cupful of their cooking water for afterwards.

Drain the pesto to the bowl.

Use a rubber spatula to completely scrape the bowl underneath the blade, acquiring all of the good pieces out. Add a few bits of the rice water because you throw the noodles and pesto together. Use a big spoon in 1 hand and the rubber spatula from the other to blend them nicely, coat the noodles in the sauce.

Serve.

Twirl tangles of pasta to shallow bowls, and spooning additional pesto along with you would like. Shower the pasta with a bit more freshly grated cheese, season with pepper and salt, and enjoy simultaneously. Leftover pasta may last up to 3 times, kept sealed from the fridge. If you stored any pesto different from the pasta, then move it into a jar and pay its surface right with plastic wrap to impede oxidation, then seal it, and then keep refrigerated for up to 1 week.

45: Butternut Mac 'n' Cheese

PREP TIME

20 minutes

COOK TIME

50 minutes

SERVES

4

Ingredients

- 4 Tbsp butter, divided, plus more for greasing ramekins
- 2 thick slices rustic bread, crusts removed and Ripped into bite-size pieces
- 1/2 Tsp kosher salt, and a hefty pinch
- 12 Oz macaroni
- 1/2 butternut squash, peeled, seeded, and Chopped into inch-long bite-size Bits
- 2 cups of milk
- 3 Tbsp all-purpose flour
- 1/4 Tsp freshly grated nutmeg
- 1/4 Tsp freshly ground black pepper
- 1/4 Tsp cayenne pepper

- 1 1/2 cups grated sharp white Cheddar cheese, divided
- 1 cup grated Gruyère cheese, Split

TOOLS / EQUIPMENT

- Box grater
- 4 ramekins
- Toaster dishwasher
- Little saucepan
- Large kettle
- Colander
- Steamer basket
- Tongs
- Whisk
- Baking sheet
- Ladle
- Wire cooling rack

Get ready the ramekins.

Steak 4 ramekins, and put aside on a baking sheet.

Toast bread.

Put the bread onto a toaster oven. In a small sauce pan moderate heat, melt 1 tablespoon of butter, then drizzle the butter onto the breadthen stirring the pieces across the menu to the jacket. Toast the croutons until lightly crispy, about five minutes, and put a side.

Cook the pasta.

Establish a massive pot filled with water on high heat and bring this to a boil. Add 1 tbsp salt, adding the pasta, and then stir fry well. Cook three minutes beneath the package instructions say, or so the pasta out is cooked as well as the inner will probably be underdone. Transfer the pasta to a colander, then shake it a few

Times to empty well. Scrub the pasta lightly to block it from cooking and put a side.

Steam the skillet.

Combine a steamer basket in a sauce pan and add 1 inch of water. Cover and steam the skillet until slightly softened, 3 to five minutes. Use tongs to remove the skillet from the jar, then rinse under hot water, then set a side.

Preheat the oven to 375°F.

Create the béchamel.

In a small sauce pan medium-low heat, then warm the milk. At the same kettle you useful for cooking the pasta, then on medium heat, melt the remaining 3 tablespoons of butter. If the butter foams, add the bread. Whisk the flour into the egg, stirring to completely combine.

Keep on whisking.

Gently pour in the milk. After massaging slide before mix doesn't need any bumps, then gently add the others of the Whisk always, until the mixture bubbles and becomes overly thick, 8 to 10 minutes.

Blend the ingredients.

Remove the pan from heat, and stir in the salt, nutmeg, black pepper, and cayenne pepper, 1 cup of Cheddar cheese, additionally 1/2 cup of Gruyère.

Add pasta and skillet.

Pour the cooked pasta and pasta skillet into the smoky béchamel sauce. Ladle the mixture into the ramekins. Squeeze the remainder 1/2 cup of Cheddar cheese and 1/2 cup of Gruyère over the tops, then arrange the refrigerated croutons as well as Bake before surfaces are golden, roughly 25 minutes.

Serve.

Transfer the casseroles to a wire cooling rack, and let cool for five minutes. Drink the small mac and cheese ramekins sexy on big plates.

46: Pan-Roasted Fish

PREP TIME

5 minutes

COOK TIME

10 minutes

SERVES

4

Ingredients

- 4 (5-ounce) skin-on fish fillets (such as red snapper, flounder, haddock, or Poultry), 1/2 into 1 inch thick
- Kosher salt
- Freshly ground black pepper
- 4 Tbsp olive oil
- 3 Tbsp butter
- 3 fresh thyme sprigs, leaves stripped from stems, coarsely chopped
- Chopped fresh parsley and lemon wedges (optional), for garnish

TOOLS / EQUIPMENT

- Big cast
- iron skillet
- Metal spatula

Prep and year the fillets.

Pat the fish dry with paper towels and season on both sides with pepper and salt.

Sauté the bass.

Put a sizable skillet over high heat. When the skillet is hot, then put in the oil. Set the fillets skin-side away from you to the pan, therefore if any splattering occurs, you will have less chance of being burnt. Press down softly using a metal spatula for approximately 20 seconds round the edges so the fillets do not flake out.

Reduce the heat and continue to cook.

Reduce the heat to moderate and let sizzle till the bass is caramelized and getting opaque round the borders, 2-3 minutes. Gently turn the fillets into the next side, and then add the rosemary and butter into the pan.

Baste the bass.

Tilt the pan slightly to swimming the peanut butter on both sides. Use a spoon to baste the fish with all the melted butter. Baste the fillets differently, till they're golden all over and cooked through, 1 minute or so, based on the depth of your bass.

Serve.

Drink immediately, with chopped coriander and lemon wedges, if desired.

47: Hearty Greens Strata

PREP TIME

15 minutes plus 2 hours to soak and 30 minutes to sit

COOK TIME

30 minutes

SERVES

4–6

Ingredients

- Olive oil, Such as sautéing
- 1 medium onion, Sliced
- 1 bunch Swiss chard or Spinach, Stalks removed and finely chopped, leaves coarsely chopped
- 1/4 Tsp freshly grated nutmeg
- Freshly ground black pepper
- Kosher salt
- 5 eggs
- 1 cup buttermilk
- 1/2 cup whole milk
- 1 Tbsp Dijon mustard

- 11/2 cups grated Gruyère cheese
- 1 cup finely shredded Parmesan
- cheese, for greasing
- 5 pieces day-old bread, then cut into big cubes
- 1 tsp red pepper flakes

Yummy additions

Sautéed and additional into the mixture:

- Broccoli
- Leeks
- Mushrooms
- Tomatoes
- Zucchini

TOOLS / EQUIPMENT

- Box grater
- Large skillet
- Moderate bowl
- Whisk
- Medium ceramic or glass
- Baking dish
- Baking sheet

Sauté veggies and aromatics.

Into a massive skillet over moderate heat, drizzle enough olive oil to coat the skillet. Add the onionand sauté until tender, 5 to 5 minutes. Insert the chard stalks and peppermint, and season with pepper and salt. Stir to include, cooking for the next two to three minutes.

Add the greens and keep cooking.

Add the chard leaves, then combine with all the other components, and then sauté till the leaves have wilted approximately two minutes. Transfer the mix to a plate.

Whisk the egg mix.

In a medium bowlwhisk together the eggs, buttermilk, milk, and walnut.

Combine the cakes.

In a shallow dish, then throw both pieces of cheese together. Put aside a third of the cheese to closing pruning before the strata enter the oven.

Twist the strata.

Steak a medium baking dish nicely. Organize a layer of cubed bread. Do not be too fussy, a modest textural inconsistency can result in sweet, salty custard layers when the strata are already cooked. Insert a layer of this onion-greens mix. Spread a layer of cheese on the surface. Repeat with every, finishing the surface with the rest bread along with a dab of red pepper aromas.

Saturate the strata.

Gently pour the egg mixture evenly across the entire face to saturate the bread layers. Permit the bread to absorb the mix for a minimum of two hours, preferably overnight. In case it stands overnight, then cover in plastic wrap and refrigerate.

Get ready yourself to bake.

Permit the strata to sit down at room temperature for 30 minutes before baking.

Preheat the oven to 350°F.

Bake the strata.

Scatter the reserved cheese on top. Put the strata onto a baking sheet and bake uncovered for half an hour, or until golden and place in the middle.

Serve.

Cool for 10 minutes and then serve while still hot. Leftover strata could be stored, refrigerated, for up to 5 times and can be reheated in the toaster oven.

48: Tomato Soup with Broiled Cheesy Toasts

PREP TIME

10 minutes

COOK TIME

35 minutes

TOTAL TIME

1 hour

SERVES

4

Ingredients

- 4 cups Berries (6 to 8 medium tomatoes), Buds peeled, Sliced
- 1 Tbsp olive oil, plus additional for drizzling
- 2 Tbsp butter 1 medium onion, Sliced
- 1/2 Tsp freshly grated nutmeg
- 1/2 Tsp smoked paprika

- Sea salt
- Freshly ground black pepper
- 2 cups chicken stock

For Those TOASTS

- 4 pieces country loaf
- 1/2 cup grated Gruyère cheese

TOOLS / EQUIPMENT

- Box grater
- Paring knife
- Moderate saucepan
- Slotted spoon
- Big bowl
- Dutch oven
- Immersion
- grinder
- spoon
- oven
- Ladle

Blanch the tomatoes and peel off the skins.

Decide on a medium saucepan full of water. Together with your knife, cut an"X" to the bottoms of these berries. Carefully lower two berries to the water at one time and blanch for 1 second. Use a slotted spoon to transfer the blanched berries into a huge bowl full of ice water. When cool enough to handle, peel off the skins and drop then slice the tomatoes into big balls over a bowl to gather your juices. Repeat with the rest of the berries, and put them into the bowl.

Create the soup.

In a pitcher or other heavy-bottomed kettle over moderate heat, warm the oil and butterand swirl the pan to coat. Sauté the onion till translucent, 5 to 5 minutes. Add the berries and their juiceand bring them to a boil. Reduce the heat, and simmer, stirring occasionally, for approximately 5 minutes.

Contain the spices and inventory, and keep cooking.

Insert the cumin and paprika, season with pepper and salt, and then put in the stock. Stir to include, go back the heat to moderate, and bring about bubbling again. Reduce the heat and simmer with the lid on for 20 to 25 minutes.

Purée the soup.

Remove the kettle from the heat, then take off the lid and let cool for 15 minutes. Pulse an immersion blender to purée the soup. Constantly maintain the blender completely submerged in the liquid whilst puréeing to prevent a huge wreck, and most significant, to prevent being burnt. Blend thoroughly to get a creamy consistency, even not as if you like it chunky.

Create grilled toasts.

Toast the bread in a toaster oven until crispy, about 5 minutes. Split the grated cheese evenly between the pieces, twist the toaster oven to broil, go back the toasts, and then simmer until the cheese is melted and bubbling, about 3 minutes longer.

Serve.

Ladle the soup into bowls, and top with all the cheesy toasts. Drizzle with olive oil, add honey and consume simultaneously.

49: Chicken Skewer Sandwiches

PREP TIME

20 minutes, plus overnight to marinate

COOK TIME

20 minutes

SERVES

4

Ingredients

- 2/3 cup olive oil, plus additional for drizzling
- 1/3 cup red wine vinegar
- 2 lemon, juiced, and Also a Single zested
- 4 garlic cloves, sliced 1 Tbsp fresh coriander leaves
- 1 Tbsp fresh oregano leaves
- 1 Tbsp fresh basil leaves, Wrapped and chiffonaded
- 1 Tsp red pepper flakes, or to taste
- 1 bay leaf
- 1 Tsp cane sugar

- 1 Tsp kosher salt1 tsp freshly ground black pepper
- 1 lb boneless chicken thighs, cut to 11/2-inch cubes
- 1 baguette, cut into 4 segments, each split lengthwise
- 1 tbsp chopped fresh mint or parsley, or a mixture, for garnish

TOOLS / EQUIPMENT

- Citrus reamer
- Zester
- Bread knife
- Big bowl
- Skewers
- Tongs
- Grill pan

Create a marinade.

In a big bowl, stir together the olive oil, lemon, lemon juice and zest, coriander, peppermint, peppermint, basil, red pepper flakes, bay leaf, salt, sugar, and pepper. Add the cubed chicken and refrigerate, covered closely or inside a large, resealable bag, overnight to marinate.

Grill the skewers.

Thread the chicken on skewers, carrying the beef itself to skewer if it's uneven. Heat a skillet over high heat till warm. Grill the chicken for about 3 to 5 minutes each side, until cooked and simmer spots.

Grill the bread.

Transfer the grilled skewers into a massive plate as you consume the bread. Drizzle olive oil on the bread and grill for about 3 to five minutes, rotating as necessary, until blackened in spots.

Serve.

These skewers are yummy laid in addition to the grilled bread using a dab of sliced fresh herbs--such as mint or parsley --to garnish.

50: Winter White Bean Stew

PREP TIME

20 minutes

plus 6 hours to soak

COOK TIME

1 hour

SERVES

4–6

Ingredients

- 3 cups Dried white beans, like cannellini, flageolet, or Underground Legumes, or a Mixture
- Two bay leaves
- Two Parmigiano-Reggiano rinds or Two Little Parmesan Blend
- 1 head garlic

- 2 Tbsp olive oil, plus additional for drizzling
- 1 jalapeño
- Kosher salt
- Freshly ground black pepper
- 2 small onions, chopped 5 to 7 Little carrots, Sliced
- 3 celery stalks, chopped
- 1 tbsp finely chopped fresh rosemary quills
- 1 tsp red pepper flakes
- 1 cup chicken stock or water
- Crusty bread, for serving

TOOLS / EQUIPMENT

- Enormous bowl
- Dutch oven
- Aluminum transparency
- Little baking
- dish processor
- decorative spoon
- Ladle
- Rubber spatula

Get the beans.

At a big enough bowl to allow them to double volume (greater than 1, if utilizing different legumes), soak the beans that are dry in sufficient cold water to cover by at least two inches. After grilling for 6 hours or overnight, then drain and wash, then move into a Dutch oven or other big, heavy-bottomed stewpot. Wipe the jar, and place it apart.

Preheat the oven to 375°F.

Cook the beans.

Put the stewpot over high heat and add sufficient water to cover the beans with at least two inches. Add the bay leaves and cheese rindsand deliver the water to a boil. When the water has been bubbling, reduce the heat, then cook the beans onto a very low simmer for about 45 minutes in one houruntil the beans are tender.

Roast the garlic along with jalapeño.

While the beans cook, then cut the top third from the thoughts of garlic. Nestle it at a sheet of aluminum foil, and drizzle olive oil on it. Fold the foil to seal the garlicand set it in a tiny baking dish. Do the same using the jalapeño at a tiny baking dish. Roast both at the oven for as long as you cook the beansthen remove and put aside to cool.

Transfer the beans along with sautéing the veggies.

If the beans are finished cooking, they will still seem somewhat soupy. Pull out the cheese rinds and drop, and transfer the beans back to the skillet. Season with pepper and salt, and put aside.

Cook the aromatics.

Put the pot to the burner on medium heat. Add olive oil and onions, along with sautéing, stirring periodically. As they begin to become translucent, add the celery and carrots, in addition to the lavender and red pepper flakes. Sauté, stirring occasionally, for 2 minutes. Season with pepper and salt.

Purée the beans together with the inventory along with the aromatics.

In a food processor, blend two cups of the cooked bean mix the roasted jalapeño without the stem, then the poultry stock, along with the tsp squeezed from half the mind of roasted garlic till creamy. (You are going to have a half-head of roasted garlic which may be utilized in different soups or smashed to yogurt or cream cheese and spread on toast) This mix will include the body to the final stew.

Stir to blend.

Drain the purée to the veggie kettle, alongside the bowl of legumes and the liquid, and then give it all a good stirfry.

Serve.

In case the stew has to be rewarmed, do this over medium-low warmth, then ladle the stew into wide bowls and then enjoy crusty bread. Any leftovers can be refrigerated for up to 1 week, or frozen for as many as two months.

51: Fresh Fish Tacos

PREP TIME

15 minutes

plus 50 minutes to marinate

COOK TIME

15 minutes

SERVES

4

Ingredients

FOR QUICK-PICKLED ONIONS

- 1/2 red onion, Chopped Lean
- Pinch black peppercorns
- 1 bay leaf
- 3/4 cup white Vinegar.

For Those TACOS

- 1 tsp cumin seeds, toasted

- 1/3 cup olive oil
- 11/2 tsp chilli powder
- 1/4 cup chopped fresh cilantro leaves, plus additional for garnish
- 1/2 into 1 jalapeño pepper, seeded and minced
- Kosher salt
- 1 lb flaky white fish (like flounder, red snapper, or cod), cut into 4 portions
- freshly ground black pepper
- 8 fresh corn or corn tortillas
- 1 recipe of Salsa Fresca or Savoy Cabbage Slaw, for serving
- Sour cream, for serving
- two limes, quartered

TOOLS / EQUIPMENT

- Small sauté pan
- Little mason jar with lid
- Mortar and pestle
- Small bowl
- Baking sheet
- Aluminum transparency
- Tea towel

Marinate the onion.

In a little mason jar with a lid, then arrange the onion pieces, including a pinch of peppercorns and a bay leaf, and pour enough white vinegar to pay. Put aside to marinate for a minimum of 30 minutes.

Marinate the bass.

Grind the toasted cumin to a coarse powder using a mortar and pestle. In a small bowlmix the olive oil, chilli powder, chopped,

chopped onions, also jalapeño, and season with salt. Set the fillets on a baking sheet and then pour the marinade over, making sure to coat the fillets nicely on either side. Marinate for 20 minutes at room temperature.

Cook the bass.

Heat the broiler using the oven rack at the maximum place. Season the fish with salt and pepper. Broil until the fillets are on top and also the flesh is opaque throughout about 5 minutes. Remove the pan in the oven and then flake the fish using a fork. Taste and adjust seasoning as necessary, then put aside.

Heat the tortillas.

Reduce the oven temperature to 400°F. Place the tortillas in 2 piles of 4, and then wrap the packages into aluminum foil. Heat in the oven for about 1 to 10 minutes, until the tortillas are heated through. Set the tortillas, still wrapped in foil, at a tea towel to keep warm.

Assemble and Serve:

To build the tacos, put a heaping spoonful of Savory Cabbage Slaw onto the Middle of a tortilla. Add the flaked fish and Salsa Fresca, and shirt with the crispy onions. Drink followed by cilantro sprigs, sour cream, and lime wedges.

52: Miso-Grilled Shrimp Skewers

PREP TIME

20 minutes plus 20 minutes to marinate

COOK TIME

5–7 minutes

SERVES

4

Ingredients

- 2 Tbsp freshly squeezed lime juicewith Additional wedges for garnish
- 2 Tbsp mirin
- 2 tablespoons yellow miso
- 1 Tbsp sesame oil
- 1 Tbsp fresh ginger, peeled and grated
- 1 large garlic clove, finely grated
- 1 Lb large shrimp, shelled and deveined

OPTIONAL EXTRAS, FOR SERVING

- Chopped scallions

- Sunflower sprouts
- Green beans, celery along with crispy
- Sliced English or Persian cucumbers
- Salad greens
- refreshing cilantro leaves
- Cooked rice or steamed buns

TOOLS / EQUIPMENT

- Citrus reamer
- Nice grater
- Enormous bowl
- Whisk
- Grill pan
- French skewers

Create the glaze.

In a big bowlwhisk together the lime juice, mirin, miso, sesame oil, ginger, and garlic. Add the beans, and toss to coat. Let marinate for 20 minutes.

Grill the fish.

Preheat a grill pan on medium-high warmth. Thread the shrimp onto metal skewers, piercing the fish in the bottom end and in the thickest aspect of their human body to fasten. Grill the fish over medium-high heat till lightly charred and opaque, turning once, about 5 minutes.

Serve.

These grilled and white shrimp are excellent served in wheat buns with chopped fresh scallions and cilantro, more rice, or combined crispy green beans, greens, or even Oriental Cucumber Salad.

53: Spring Rolls and Dipping Sauces

PREP TIME

35 minutes

COOK TIME

5 minutes

SERVES

4

Ingredients

FOR THE DIPPING SAUCES

- 4 Tsp fish sauce
- 1/4 cup water
- 2 Tbsp freshly squeezed lime juice
- 1 small garlic clove, grated
- 1 Tsp cane sugar
- 1/2 Tsp chilli sauce (like sambal oelek); Significantly Less if you Want less spice
- 2 Tbsp crunchy peanut butter
- 4 Tbsp hoisin sauce

For Those ROLLS

- 1-ounce rice vermicelli
- Hot water, for grilling
- 8-grain wrappers (81/2-inch diameter)
- 12 large shrimp, peeled, cooked, and halved lengthwise
- 2 tablespoons fresh Thai basil leaves
- 3 tbsp fresh mint leaves
- 3 tablespoons fresh cilantro leaves
- 2 lettuce leaves (like butter or romaine), halved
- 1/2 cup mung bean sprouts
- 1 carrot, julienned

TOOLS / EQUIPMENT

- Citrus reamer
- Box grater
- 2 little bowls
- Little saucepan
- Whisk
- Medium saucepan
- Colander
- Enormous bowl
- skillet

Create the 2 sauces.

In a small bowlstir together the components to the very first sauce: fish sauce, water, carrot juice, sugar, garlic and chilli sauce. Put aside. In a small saucepan over moderate heat, mix ingredients to the next sauce: peanut butter along with hoisin sauce. Add a few spoonfuls of water to cut the sauce slightly, and then simmer till incorporated. Transfer into a different little bowl then set aside.

Prep that the vermicelli.

In a medium saucepan, then put the rice noodles in warm water until they turn clean and then soften. You'll turn to the heat to do so, but don't boil themas they might become soggy. Transfer the noodles into a colander and rinse under cold water. Drain and put aside.

Prep that the wrappers.

Have sufficient"bathwater-warm" water in a bowl big enough so that if you dip your wrappers, the water comes up halfway. Dunk and elevator, rotate a quarter-turn and repeat till you've gone all of the waysaround with all the wrapper. The time dunking takes maybe two minutes complete, as you're simply hoping to soften it. With this process, the wrapper gets pliable but is not less likely to rip.

Build the rolls.

Set the moist wrapper onto a damp dishtowel placed flat on the work surface. Organize 3 hens halves pink-side down followed by a pinch of this Thai basil, mint, and basil leaves, and then a bunch of those crispy components: lettuce, bean sprouts, and carrots, and a little couple of vermicelli, folding the span of noodles back and forth till you've got a neat heap. Leave a 2inch edge on each side since you layer the components.

Bundle the components, and then roll.

You intend to earn a tight package when rolling. Gently pull the border of the wrapper around the fillings. Gently use your hands to push on the fillings to a little package under the wrapper. Adding them right into a tiny package will keep all of the components together and assist the roster stay firm as well as.

Produce a company seal.

Roll away from you, and then transplant the fillings before you personally. After a complete rotation, then fold the sides of the wrapper in. Continue rolling up to the border, collecting fillings in till the roster is sealed.

Serve.

Spring rolls may be served complete with a skillet on the side or cut on the diagonal to exhibit their vibrant fillings. Refrigerate the final rolls up to two hours before serving, each wrapped separately in plastic wrap. The rice wrappers will toughen if kept more than a couple of hours, increasing their probability of cracking.

54: Sopa De Lima (chicken lime soup)

PREP TIME

20 minutes

COOK TIME

30 minutes

SERVES

4–6

Ingredients

- Safflower oil, for frying
- 3 corn tortillas, cut to 1/4-inch
- Pieces Flake salt, for Example Maldon
- 1 white onion, Sliced
- 4 bone-in, skinless chicken thighs
- 3 Roma tomatoes, cored
- 1 serrano or jalapeño chilli, cored, seeded, and Sliced
- 1/2 Tsp dried thyme
- 2 garlic cloves, finely grated
- 3 cups chicken stock
- Juice of 3 limes1 Also Two Slice into wedges for serving
- 11/2 cups frozen peas, blanched

- 2 Lettuce, Chopped or cubed, for garnish
- Fresh basil leaves, for garnish
- Freshly ground black pepper

TOOLS / EQUIPMENT

- Fine grater
- Citrus reamer
- Large skillet
- Tongs
- Slotted spoon
- Wire cooling rack
- Big bowl
- Ladle

Fry the tortilla pieces.

Into a large skillet, pour enough oil to ensure it includes a quarter inch. Heat the oiland when quite hot, fry the tortilla strips in tiny batches until crisp and golden, 30 minutes to 1 second per batch. Tortilla strips must flow immediately upon contact with all the acrylic, but maybe not burnoff. If the oil is smoking, then reduce the heat.

Move the tortilla pieces.

Use a slotted spoon or tongs to move the fried tortillas into a paper towel-lined wire cooling rack to consume excess oil. Sprinkle with a pinch of salt. Repeat till all of the tortilla strips are fried. Put the tortilla strips apart and reserve the oil.

Sauté the onion along with the chicken.

In a large sauce pan over medium heatthen apply 1 tablespoon of the skillet to sauté the skillet till translucent, about five minutes. Add another tablespoon of the oil, and brown the chicken thighs turning to brown all sides.

Simmer the soup.

Include the berries, jalapeño, coriander, coriander, and inventory, and then make the mixture to a boil. Reduce heat to simmer and simmer for about 20 minutes, or till the fish is cooked through, breaking up the tomatoes with most of the main advantage of a wooden spoon halfway through simmering.

Shred the beef.

Remove the sauce pan from heat. Use tongs to go out the chicken of this soup into a major bowl. When cool enough to handle, discard the bones and shred the meat with the hands or using two forks. Pour the grilled chicken in to the soup, then add the carrot juice peas. Stir to combine taste, and correct the seasoning as required.

Serve.

Ladle the soup into bowls, and top with the avocado, cilantro leaves, along with fried tortillas. Squeeze the lime wedges within the soup and consume immediately. Permit any lingering soup to return to room temperature, and keep refrigerated in sealed containers for up to 3 times. Fried tortilla strips can maintain room temperature, stored between layers of parchment and sealed, for two days. Reheat tortillas from the toaster oven or even a sauté pan.

55: Roasted Chicken with Onions and Lemons

PREP TIME

10 minutes

COOK TIME

55 minutes

TOTAL TIME

1 hour, 20 minutes

SERVES

4

Ingredients

- 1 (3-to 4-pound) Entire Poultry
- Sea salt
- Freshly ground black pepper
- 1 Tbsp olive oil, plus additional for drizzling
- 4 onions, Then cut into wedges

- 5 lemons, halved 1 head garlic, Then High third cut
- 5 fresh Coriander sprigs

TOOLS / EQUIPMENT

- Large cast-iron skillet
- Tongs
- Slotted spoon
- Big plate

Preheat the oven to 425°F.

Season the chicken.

Season the entire chicken well with pepper and salt. Transform it the buttocks along with underneath the wings and over the pit.

Brown the chicken.

Heat a gigantic skillet medium-high heathen add the coconut oil and then cook the chicken, then then breast-side down, till golden brown. Use tongs together side a spoonful to lightly twist your poultry careful not to tear the epidermis. Brown on all sides, 10 to 15 minutes total, and proceed to some plate.

Prep the chicken for roasting.

In precisely the same skillet, coating the onions in the middle, so they will be under the chicken since you roast it. They'll soak up the juices and fat, which will cause them to super and tender yummy. Add the lemon wedges, cut-side right down, along with the garlic and simmer. Drizzle everything together with olive oil.

Roast the chicken.

Place the chicken back in the skillet the onion pile. Roast until a meat thermometer inserted into the thickest section of the thigh registers 165°F, 35 to 40 minutes. An extra means to learn whether the poultry is ready would be always to cut the thigh in the joint. Once the juices run clear, it's ready.

Serve.

Before cutting to the chicken, allow it to rest for 10 to 15 minutes, letting the inner juices. The chicken is excellent served together with the tender veggies. Spoon the pan juices and love!

56: Mini Pot Pies

PREP TIME

15 minutes

COOK TIME

1 hour

TOTAL TIME

1 hour, 25 minutes

SERVES

4

Ingredients

- 1 sheet frozen puff pastry, for Example, Dufour Manufacturer, thawed in the fridge
- 2 Tbsp Loaf Bread, plus Additional for dusting Top
- 4 Tbsp unsalted butter
- 1 shallot, finely chopped
- 2 Tbsp fresh thyme leaves
- 1 cup low-sodium chicken broth
- 1 cup whole milk
- Kosher salt

- Freshly ground black pepper
- 4 carrots, Peeled and Chopped
- 3 cups diced leftover turkey or chicken
- 1 cup frozen peas, thawed
- 1 cup white pearl onions, peeled
- 1/4 cup sliced fresh flat-leaf skillet
- hot sauce, to taste
- 1 egg, lightly crushed

TOOLS / EQUIPMENT

- Vegetable peeler
- Rolling trap
- Parchment paper
- Baking sheet
- Big skillet
- Whisk
- Ladle
- 4 ramekins
- Pastry brush

Preheat the oven to 400°F.

Roll the pastry out.

Unfold the pastry and roll it onto a lightly floured surface to 1/4 inch thick. Cut it equal-size bits marginally larger compared to the size of this ramekins. Lay them from parchment paper, then proceed to some baking sheet, and simmer until ready to utilize it.

Create the roux.

At a large skillet over medium heat, warm the egg. If it's melted and simmer, add the shallot and cook and simmer till the shallot becomes translucent, about 4 minutes, stirring often. Insert the bread and cook, stirring frequently, until the mixture is gold and completely incorporated, about five minutes.

Add the rest of the ingredients.

Whisk in the broth including the very first half before adding the others. Whisk in the milkand season with salt and pepper. Bring to a boil, then reduce heat and simmer, whisking occasionally, until the mixture is still thick enough to coat a spoon, then 10 to 12 minutes. Add the carrots and cook till just tender, 3 to five minutes. Insert the chicken, peas, onions, and simmer year with hot sauce, salt, and pepper and stir to combine.

Get ready the ramekins.

Ladle the mixture into 4 ramekins or mini casseroles assembled with a sterile sheet. Drape puff pastry over filling, therefore making certain it hangs within ramekin borders. Gently press on the borders. Brush the pastry with the beaten egg and get a slit at the centers utilizing a sharp knife to find steam to escape while baking.

Bake the pot pops.

Bake until the puffpastry surfaces are golden as well as the filling is wrapped throughout the slits, 15 to 20 minutes. Reduce heat to 350°F, then consume till the puffpastry is profoundly gold and cooked through, 10 to 15 minutes longer.

Serve.

Let sit 10 minutes before serving on big plates.

57: Turkey Pan Bagnat

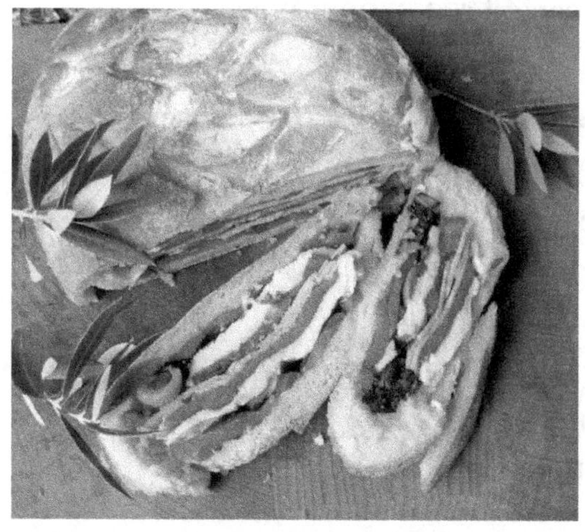

PREP TIME

15 minutes plus 20 minutes to weight down

COOK TIME

none

SERVES

4

Ingredients

FOR THE DRESSING

- 2 Tbsp Dijon mustard
- 1 Tbsp mayonnaise
- 1 Tsp red wine vinegar
- 1/4 cup chopped fresh parsley
- 1 Tbsp olive oil

FOR THE SANDWICH

- 1 (10-inch) loaf ciabatta bread
- 1 couple haricots verts, blanched, cut to bite-size bits
- 1 cup roasted red pepper pieces
- 1/2 little red onion, chopped lean
- Flake salt, like Maldon
- Freshly ground black pepper
- 8 ounces thinly sliced roasted turkey breast
- 1/2 cup pesto

TOOLS / EQUIPMENT

- Small bowl
- Bread knife
- Whisk
- Plastic wrapping
- Cast-iron skillet

Make the dressing table.

In a small bowlwhisk together the mustard, mustard, vinegar, parsley, and olive oil. Put aside.

Build the sandwich.

Slice the ciabatta in half. Gently hollow out the ground half and place it on vinyl wrap large enough to roll the sandwich. Put a layer of all these about the bread inside this sequence: dressing table, haricots verts, roasted pepper, and chopped onion. Season with pepper and salt. Drizzle the dressing over, then put in the turkey.

Weight the sandwich down.

Distribute the top with pesto, put it to your sandwich, and then wrap closely. Place the toaster at a resealable plastic bag, squeezing out any air before sealing. Put a skillet over the sandwich to press 10 minutes. Switch the sandwich and press it back for another 10 minutes.

Serve.

Before serving, remove the pounds, unwrap the sandwichand let it come to room temperature, or maintain it wrapped and optional in the fridge for half an hour or overnight. This excess time allows the flavours to meld. Cut into four segments.

58: Pulled Pork Sliders

PREP TIME

15 minutes plus 1 hour to rest

COOK TIME

3 hours, 40 minutes

TOTAL TIME

5 hours, 15 minutes

SERVES

8

Ingredients

- 2 Tsp whole coriander seeds
- 2 Tsp whole cumin seeds
- 2 Tbsp dark brown sugar
- 1 Tbsp kosher salt
- 1 Tsp freshly ground black pepper
- 1 Tbsp paprika 1 Teaspoon
- 1/2 Tsp dry mustard powder
- 1/4 teaspoon ground cayenne pepper

- 1 (6-to 8-pound) bone-in beef shoulder, rather skin-on
- 1/2 cup apple cider vinegar
- 2 tbsp cane sugar
- Pinch red pepper flakes
- Toasted buns, for serving
- 1 recipe Savory Cabbage Slaw (here), for serving

TOOLS / EQUIPMENT

- Small cast-iron skillet
- Mortar and pestle
- Small bowl
- Plastic wrapping
- Tray
- Aluminum transparency
- Baking sheet
- Big bowl
- Tongs

Toast the spices.

In a tiny, ironic cast-iron skillet over moderate heat, toast the coriander and simmer until aromatic, about 1 to 2 minutes. Work with a mortar and pestle to grind the skillet to some powder.

Build the flavour.

In a small bowlmix the brown sugar, pepper, salt, coriander, cumin, paprika, mustard powder, and cayenne, mixing with your hands or a fork until well blended.

Season the beef and allow it to break.

Rub the spice mix over the whole surface of the pork, then caking just like a lot of it on the meat as possible. In case you have time, allow the meat rest 1 to 2 hours at room temperature before cooking, then refrigerate immediately, neatly wrapped in plastic and then place onto a tray.

Preheat the oven to 325°F.

But adjust the oven rack into the lower-middle place.

Roast the pork.

Put the pork on a foil-lined, rimmed baking sheet, then skin-side-up, and simmer for 3 to 2 31/2 hoursor till the beef is more pull-apart tender.

Let it break.

Transfer the pork into a large bowland let it rest at least 20 minutes.

Roast the skin.

Use tongs to carefully raise off the skin. Raise the oven temperature to 500°F. Use a fork to scratch some clinging meat to the bowl. Remove the fat in the skin and drop, returning the epidermis into the baking sheet. Roast skin for 5 to 10 minutes, until smooth and bubbly. Remove from the oven and place aside.

Shred the meat.

Shred the pork with two forks or your palms. Save for stock or drop. Finely chop your epidermis, and blend it with the meat, eliminating any visible fat. Season the beef with pepper and salt. Stir the vinegar, cane sugar, and a pinch of red pepper and increase the mix to flavour.

Serve.

Drink the pork sexy, piled on toasted buns and topped with Savory Cabbage Slaw. Store the pork for up to 4 times refrigerated in a sealed jar. Also, it stays suspended for up to 1 month.

59: Minty Lamb Burgers

PREP TIME

10 minutes

COOK TIME

12–15 minutes

SERVES

4

Ingredients

- 11/2 pounds ground lamb
- 1 garlic clove, finely grated
- 3 Tbsp finely chopped fresh mint
- 3 Tbsp finely chopped fresh parsley
- 1/2 Tsp cumin seeds, toasted and ground in a mortar and pestle
- Kosher salt
- Freshly ground black pepper
- Olive oil, for brushing
- Ciabatta rolls, for serving

- Easy Tzatziki, for serving
- Romaine lettuce leaves, for serving

Yummy additions

- Feta cheese, chopped lean
- Red onion, sliced thin

TOOLS / EQUIPMENT

- Fine grater
- Medium bowl
- Pastry brush
- Grill pan
- Tongs
- Bread knife

Create the patties.

In a medium bowl, lightly mix the butter with garlic, mint, parsley, cumin, and a pinch each of salt and pepper. Split the beef into 4 patties of equal size and depth --roughly 1/2 inch thick--and then move to a plate. Press a little dimple in the middle of each patty using 2 palms to cancel the way that it shrinks as it cooks. Gently brush the hamburgers with olive oiland season again with salt and pepper.

Cook the burgers.

Heat the skillet on high heat. If it is warm, brush the grate gently with olive oil. Grill the patties over medium heat for 2 to 8 minutes to get medium-rare approximately 2 to 10 minutes for medium, turning halfway through. Transfer them to a plate.

Grill the bread.

Slice the ciabatta in half, brush lightly with olive oil, and then put cut-side down to the skillet pan. Grill long enough to enable the bread into charin stains, 3 to 5 minutes.

Serve.

Set the bread and top with all the hamburgers. Garnish with all the Easy Tzatziki, romaine, and also some other yummy additions.

60: Savory Beef Ragù

PREP TIME

15 minutes

COOK TIME

1 hour 40 minutes

SERVES

4

Ingredients

- 2 Bits thick-cut bacon, diced
- 1 onion, Sliced
- 2 carrots, scrubbed and Sliced
- 2 celery stalks, Sliced
- 4 garlic cloves, finely grated
- 1 fennel bulb, sliced
- 3 anchovy fillets
- 1 Lb ground beef
- 1/2 cup dry red wine

- 2 fresh thyme sprigs, leaves stripped from stems
- 1 bay leaf
- 1/2 Tsp red chilli flakes
- ⅛ Tsp freshly grated nutmeg
- ⅛ Tsp ground cinnamon
- 1 Cup (28-ounce) can whole plum tomatoes
- 1 Tbsp tomato paste
- 1 cup beef stock
- 2 Tsp balsamic vinegar
- 2 Tsp Worcestershire sauce
- Kosher salt
- Freshly ground black pepper

TOOLS / EQUIPMENT

- Fine grater
- Dutch oven
- decorative spoon

Cook the bacon.

In an oven or alternative heavy-bottomed pot over medium heat, then cook the bacon until just crispy, approximately seven minutes. Take out the bacon from your fat, and put a side.

Cook the veggies.

Sauté the onion in the bacon fat until translucent, stirring occasionally, about 10 minutes. Add the carrots and celery, stir to combine, and cook another five minutes until lightly browned. Add the garlic, peppermint, and anchovies, helping to make a very small bit at the base of the pot for all those anchovies. While they begin to sizzle, split up the anchovies up with all of the main advantage of a wooden spoon and stir to add.

Add the remaining ingredients.

Add the ground beef and bacon into the pot. Sauté until lightly browned, 5 to 7 minutes, stirring and breaking meat up as potential failed the anchovies. Add your wine because it rollsscrapes the bottom of this pot to absorb some browned pieces. Reduce the wine by 30 minutes stirring periodically, and then add the thyme, bay leaf, chili peppermint, peppermint, cinnamon, tomatoes, tomato paste, beef stock, vinegar, and Worcestershire sauce. Give an excellent stir to supply the exact mixture together.

Bring the ragù into a simmer.

Taste, season with salt and pepper necessary as well as also insure. Turn heat to low so that it bubbles gently. After 10 minutes or so, split the softened berries to chunks utilising the benefit of a wooden spoon.

Proceed to simmer.

Cover and simmer for another 45 minutes to 1 hour until the components hold the sauce has thickened. Season with salt and pepper.

Serve

Serve hot straight from the bud place on a trivet in the dining table. This dish is excellent tossed with pasta or alongside crusty bread.

Desserts

Being healthy does not mean that you cannot eat --a more balanced diet usually means you could eat a lot of items but in moderation. In reality, dessert is a perfect chance to get more fruit in your diet plan! Just remember cakes and desserts may be high in fat, so eat wisely. There is something for everybody within this part, from sour gelatin to crunchy cobbler, also out of tasty popsicles to apple cakes. Here are a few simpler tips for yummy desserts to attempt.

61: Dreamy Cheesecake

PREP TIME

20 minutes plus 3 hours to chill

COOK TIME

1 hour

SERVES

10

Ingredients

FOR THE CRUST

- 1 Package Entire wheat graham crackers (9 crackers)
- 1 Tsp ground cinnamon
- 3 Tbsp cane sugar
- 1/2 Tsp kosher salt
- 1/3 cup butter, melted

FOR THE CAKE

- two (8-ounce) packages cream cheese, at room temperature
- 1/4 tsp pure vanilla extract

- 1 tsp finely grated lemon zest
- 11/4 cups cane sugar
- 2 tsp all-purpose flour
- 1/4 tsp kosher salt
- 5whole eggs, plus 1 egg yolk
- 1/4 cup heavy cream

TOOLS / EQUIPMENT

- Zester
- Resealable bag
- bumping trap
- Moderate bowl
- Rubber spatula
- Springform pan
- Electric mixer
- Enormous bowl
- Little bowl
- Baking sheet

Create the crust.

Place the graham crackers to a resealable plastic tote. Utilizing a rolling pin, crush the crackers to crumbs. In the event that you'd preferably a nicer crust, then then keep beating the crackers until you've achieved a feel you would like. At a medium bowl blend the crushed graham crackers, cinnamon salt and sugar. Pour at the skillet and stir to combine.

Type and place the crust.

Use a rubber spatula or the back of a spoon spread and compress the mix evenly into a 9-inch springform pan. Press the crust a bit of the side of this pan, making sure that the crust is at its foundation and thins because it moves up. Chill in the fridge to place as you make the filling.

Preheat the oven to 500°F.

Mix the meeting.

In a big bowlbeat the cheese with an electric mixer till fluffy. Add the vanilla and lemon peel, and mix to blend.

Blend the remaining ingredients.

In a small bowlstir together the sugar, bread, and salt. Gently combine the dry ingredients to the cheese. One at a time, put in the eggs and also extra yolk, then whipping to blend and then pausing after every to scratch the sides of the jar. Gently include the lotion, and mix to blend.

Bake the cake.

Pour the mixture in to the crust. Placed onto the baking sheet, and bake for 5 to 6 minutes. Minimize the temperature to 200°F, and then inhale for about 45 to 55 minutes more, before the borders are gold and the center still jiggles. Flip off the oven, along with additionally the door ajar, enable the noodle to chill inside for around a hour. Refrigerate for a couple of weeks to instantly.

Serve.

Take out the cake from the fridge. Operate a butter knife round the interior border to loosen the cake at the pan. Open up the springform panthen get rid of the cake, and then function at an identical moment.

62: Flognarde (apple-custard bake)

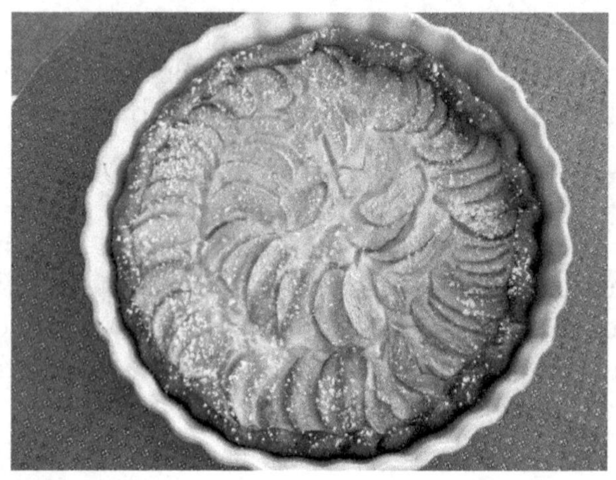

PREP TIME

15 minutes

COOK TIME

30 minutes

SERVES

4

Ingredients

- 4 Tbsp butter, cubed, and more for greasing the pan
- 5 Tbsp flour
- 4 Tbsp sugar
- Zest of 2 Meyer lemons
- 2/3 cup whole milk
- 4 eggs
- 3 apples, peeled, cored, and cut to 1/2-inch Legumes
- Confectioners' sugarfor dusting

TOOLS / EQUIPMENT

- Zester
- Vegetable peeler
- Large cast-ironskillet
- Moderate bowl
- Whisk

Grease the pan.

Steak a skillet that is homogenous.

Preheat the oven to 400°F.

Mix the components:

In a medium bowlmix the yogurt, sugar, lemon zest, and also milk. Add the eggs and beat harshly. Keep on whisking as you pour the mix to the pan.

Organize the fruit.

Fan the apple wedges and then put them on the mix. It is ok if they slip a bit as you organize them.

Bake the custard.

Dot the surface with butterand bake until the custard puffs and has become golden brown at the edges, about thirty minutes.

Serve.

Dust confectioners' sugar on the custard. Serve warm or at room temperature, then cut into wedges.

63: Peach-Blueberry Crisp

PREP TIME

10 minutes

COOK TIME

45 minutes

TOTAL TIME

1 hour 15 minutes

SERVES

4

Ingredients

- 2/3 cup Chopped oats
- 1/3 cup packed brown sugarplus 3 Tbsp of fruit
- 1/4 cup and 2 Tbsp Loaf Bread, Split
- 1/2 Tsp ground cinnamon
- 2 Tbsp fresh ginger, finely Chopped Kosher salt
- 3/4 stick butter, freezer-cold and cubed
- 2 pounds peaches or nectarines, cut into thin wedges
- 2 cups blueberries
- 2 Tsp freshly squeezed lemon juice
- 1 Tsp lemon zest

TOOLS / EQUIPMENT

- Zester
- Citrus reamer
- 2 big bowls
- glass or ceramic
- baking dish
- Baking sheet
- Wire cooling rack

Mix the dry skin.

In a major bowlthen stir with a fork to combine the ginger, then 1/3 cup of brownish sugar1/4 cup along with a tablespoon of bread, together side all the cinnamon. Insert the ginger, a pinch of salt as well as the egg in to the mixture, and work the egg into the dry ingredients with your palms before pea-size grinds remain. Refrigerate.

Preheat the oven to 375°F.

Mix the berry.

In another bowlstir together the blueberries and peaches together with the lemon juice and simmer, the remaining 3 tbsp of brown sugar, the remaining tbsp of flour, and a pinch of salt. Toss all to unite.

Bake the sharp.

Pour the orange mix into a baking dish, then then twist on the oat mix along with all the coat. In the baking sheet, then and then inhale the sharp until the topping is golden and the juices bubble, then then 30 to 4-5 seconds. Enable the sharp to cool on a wire cooling rack to get 20 or more minutes.

Serve.

The sharp would be delicious served hot, room space, as well as cold. It is so virtuous you can eat it for dinner! This sweet number is exceptional by itself, but it will be excellently wrapped with ice cream.

64: Chocolate-Pomegranate Brownies

PREP TIME

10 minutes

COOK TIME

30 minutes

TOTAL TIME

50 minutes

MAKES

12

Ingredients

- 12 ounces semisweet dark chocolate (like Callebaut), Sliced, divided
- 11/2 sticks butter, cut into cubes
- 4 eggs
- 11/4 cup light brown sugar
- 1 cup Whole-wheat Bread

- Seeds from 1/2 New pomegranate, for topping

TOOLS / EQUIPMENT

- Dual boiler
- Rubber spatula
- Parchment paper
- Baking dish
- Big bowl
- Electric mixer
- Skewer or toothpick
- Wire cooling rack

Preheat the oven to 350°F.

Melt the chocolate.

With a double boiler, melt the chocolate and the butter. Be cautious that the water does not bubble up to the top saucepan since you do this, or it'll destroy the chocolate. Eliminate the melted chocolate pan in the warm water tub, wipe out the base with a sterile dish towel to guarantee no pops, stir the butter-chocolate blend together, and put aside.

Prep the baking dish.

Line a square or little square baking dish with parchment long that the newspaper extends beyond borders by a minimum of two inches on either side.

Mix the remaining ingredients.

In a big bowl, use a fork or hand mixer to completely blend the eggs, sugarand bread. Insert the somewhat cooled, melted chocolate mixture and the remaining part of chopped chocolate, stirring to blend.

Bake the brownies.

Pour the mix to the prepared baking dish, and bake for 25 minutes, or until a skewer or toothpick comes out nearly clean. If you like the tin, then the centre should proceed only a little.

Allow the rest of the brownie.

Cool the brownies onto a wire cooling rack for 10 minutes on the pan; afterward, employing the parchment tabs on both sides and lift the brownies out.

Serve.

Cut the brownies into squaresand scatter the pomegranate seeds in addition to enjoy the yummy combination of still-molten chocolate and sour, juicy pomegranate!

65: Coconut Ice Pops

PREP TIME

10 minutes

plus 4 hours to freeze

COOK TIME

none

SERVES

4–8

Ingredients

- 3 (5.4 Oz) cans unsweetened organic coconut cream
- Juice and finely grated zest of 1 Teaspoon
- 1/3 cup maple syrup or honey

TOOLS / EQUIPMENT

- Zester
- Food blender or processor
- Rubber spatula
- Ice pop moulds or small paper cups
- Cosmetic ice-pop sticks
- Bobby hooks

Blend these components.

In a food processor, purée the coconut lotion, lime zest and juiceand maple syrup.

Prep the ice pops.

Twist on the puréed mix into moulds or little paper cups. Add wooden icepop sticks, then clipping bobby pins into the sticks and then placing them around the mould to anchor the rods set up.

Allow the ice pops upset.

Freeze the pops up for 4 hours.

Serve.

To unmold, should using paper cups, then simply peel away the paper and consume. If using ice pop moulds, then run under warm water.

66: Very Berry Trifle

PREP TIME

20 minutes plus 1 hour to chill

COOK TIME

none

SERVES

4

Ingredients

- 3 cups mixed berries of your choice
- 5 Tbsp cane sugardivided
- Juice of 1 lemon
- Juice of 1/2 orange
- 1 cup mascarpone
- 2 cups heavy whipping cream
- 1/4 Tsp pure vanilla extract
- Pinch kosher salt
- 8 ounces Soda, pound cake, or ladyfingers, sectioned into 1/2-inch Pieces to fit into Eyeglasses

TOOLS / EQUIPMENT

- Citrus reamer
- Medium bowl
- big bowl
- Electrical mixer
- Rubber spatula
- 4 eyeglasses
- Vinyl wrap

Wipe the berries.

In a medium bowl, soak the berries in half of the sugar and the orange and lemon juices. Allow the blend soften for 10 minutes since you prep the lotion.

Create the whipped cream.

In a big bowlwhisk together the mascarpone, thick cream, vanilla extract, then the residual two 1/2 tbsp of sugar, along with the salt until soft peaks form. It is possible to speed up the process by using a product, but doing this by hand must take just a couple of minutes, as a result of the abundant body of this mascarpone.

Build the trifle.

In 4 short cylindrical or wide-mouth eyeglasses, organize the ladyfingers or dessert bits to cover at the bottom. Spoon the berry mix on the cake at an even coating. Use a rubber spatula to spread the whipped cream layer in addition to the fruit, then holding the glass and then turning it into your hands as you distribute the lotion. Repeat layering every glass: berry, cake mix, and lotion, a few times before the glasses are extremely complete, finish with the cream at the top. Chill, covered in plastic wrap, for 1 to 3 weeks.

Serve.

Serve sprinkled with strands long enough to attain at the base of all of the layers, and love. Yum!

67: Banana "ice cream"

PREP TIME

7 minutes, plus 1 hour to freeze

COOK TIME

none

SERVES

4

Ingredients

- 1 Pack (5--8) ripe but firm bananas
- Pinch kosher salt

Yummy additions

- Berries
- Greek yogurt or crème fraîche
- Ground cinnamon
- Nut butter
- Chocolate

TOOLS / EQUIPMENT

- Baking sheet
- Food processor
- Rubber spatula

Prep the carrots.

Peel the carrots and cut them to high heeled coins. Freeze for 1 to 2 hours (or overnight) onto a baking sheet)

Combine the carrots.

With a food processor, combine the carrots with only a pinch of salt until they get creamy and smooth, about 5 minutes. Stop occasionally and scrape the bowl down. See the bananas change, such as magical into ice cream! If you want to incorporate in different tastes, do this today, and reunite to blend.

Serve.

For the best taste, remove it in the freezer 10 minutes before serving. Cover and freeze any leftovers. Ice cream may be made five days ahead.

68: Strawberry-Rhubarb Mini Tarts

PREP TIME

30 minutes plus 1 hour to chill

COOK TIME

45 minutes

MAKES

8

Ingredients

FOR THE DOUGH

- Two 1/2 cups all-purpose bread
- 1 tsp cane sugarplus 1 tsp for sprinkling
- 1 tsp kosher salt
- 2 sticks butter, freezer-cold and chopped into little cubes
- 1/4 cup ice water

FOR THE FILLING

- 3/4 pound rhubarb, rinsed, ends trimmed, cut 1/4-inch pieces
- 2 pints fresh strawberries, rinsed and hulled, cut to 1/4-inch bits
- 1/2 cup cane sugar

- Zest of 1 orange
- 1/4 cup orange juice
- Pinch kosher salt

TOOLS / EQUIPMENT

- Zester
- Food processor
- Plastic wrap
- Big bowl
- 2 baking sheets
- Parchment paper
- Pastry brush
- cooling rack

Create the dough.

In a food processor, combine the flour, sugar, and salt to blend. Add the cold butter and pulse 5 to seven days, till the butter blends with all the flour to make pea-size crumbs. At a slow flow, add the ice while stirring, stopping when the dough holds together.

Evaluation of the dough.

To check, unplug the food processor, open the lidand press a few doughs together. If it holds together, it is ready. If it crumbles, add a little more ice water since you pulse a couple more times. You might use less or slightly greater than 1/4 cup of plain water.

Set the dough onto a long sheet of plastic wrap.

Separate the dough into two mounds, then flatten each to make a disc. Cut the plastic wrapping in 2 between the discs, and wrap each. Refrigerate for 20 or more minutes to allow it firm up.

Create the filling.

In a big bowl, then carefully combine the rhubarb, berries, orange, orange zest, orange juice, and salt. Cover with plastic wrap, and allow the flavours meld, at least 15 minutes.

Roll the dough.

In a lightly floured surfaceand cut on every disc into four. Chill the remainder because you roll each workout. Roll in the centre to the border, turning the eighth twist with every pass of this rolling pin, until the dough is currently ⅛ inch thick. (They do not need to be perfect circles. Patch any big tears with soup pinched in the border.)

Build the tarts.

Line 2 baking sheets with parchment paper, and then put the rolled pastry 2-3 inches apart from each other. Spoon mounds of this fruit mixture to the middle of each sip, splitting the filling evenly and also than leaving a 1-inch border around the edge. Assemble 1 pair of tarts at one time, leaving another batch of crab in the fridge.

Crimp the sour edges.

Collect the pastry borders, making pleats on the stacked fruit. Gently brush water between the springs to press on the batter together and keep it in position. If the dough gets flabby, it has to be rechilled.

Refrigerate the tarts.

As soon as you've full and crimped every one of the tarts, refrigerate them for at least 1 hour before baking. Repeat steps 5 through 8 using the dough.

Preheat the oven to 400°F.

Bake the tarts.

Very softly brush the borders of the pastry with water and then scatter with the allowed 1 teaspoon of sugarfree. Waiting for 30 minutes or till the crusts are gold, then lower the temperature to 375°F and inhale for 10 to fifteen minutes before juices bubble and also the crust remains deeply golden. Move the tarts to a cable cooling rack to cool.

Serve.

Remove the tarts whenever they are readily treated, and revel in them hot. Store leftover tarts in room temperature, wrapped loosely in foil, for two days.

69: Chocolate-Cherry Bark

PREP TIME

10 minutes

plus 15 minutes to chill

COOK TIME

10 minutes

MAKES

1 SHEET

Ingredients

- 1 pound bittersweet dark chocolate, cut into small pieces
- 2 cups granola of the choice
- 1 cup dried sour cherries, coarsely chopped
- Flake salt, for Example Maldon

TOOLS / EQUIPMENT

- Dual boiler
- Parchment paper
- Baking sheet
- Rubber spatula

Prep the chocolate along with the pan.

In a double boiler, melt the chocolate. Put parchment paper on a baking sheetand put the granola to a heap on it.

Mix the bark collectively.

When the chocolate is flashed, pour it on the granola, and with a rubber spatula, blend both completely. As you blend, disperse the chocolate-covered granola in an even layer in the baking sheet. Keep spreading before the mix reaches the borders, end up roughly 1/4 inch thick.

Insert the salty and sweet accents.

Scatter the chopped pulp around, pressing them gently into the bark, then scatter the salt. Utilize the salt as an accent over a floor cover.

Allow the bark Collection.

Put the baking sheet at a cool place. Refrigerate for 15 minutes should you would rather accelerate its cooling. Split the mix into bits. Refrigerate in a sealed container to put away.

Serve.

Eliminate the bark in the fridge half an hour before serving to enable the flavours to fully blossom. Serve on a dish. It retains for two weeks, refrigerated--even if it lasts that long!

Smoothies and Beverages

If you haven't created a smoothie or enjoyable drink at home, Now's the time to try it. You'll require a blender for a number of those beverages, and the majority of them taste finest at a fine, tall glass. But these are the only principles! You can use fruit, yogurt, ice cream, juice, milk... Whatever seems like it may taste good. (And as they're mostly just one serving, in case your mixture is not so great, you have not wasted a lot on your experiment) Smoothies and backpacks are all simple to make and so delicious to taste. As soon as you've tried one as a breakfast beverage or after-practice bite, then they might only become your next favourite treat!

70: Cinnamon-Raisin Smoothie

Ingredients

- Moderate carrotspeeled - 4 per
- Moderate bananas - Two per
- Ground cinnamon - Two Tsp
- Raisins - 1 Tbsp
- Unsweetened almond milk - 2 cups
- Ice 1 cup OR filtered water - 1/2 cup
- Garnish: Ingredients

Method:

Put all of the ingredients, except the garnish in a blender. Begin lower, then boost the rate. Mix until smooth.

Garnish:

Topoff every glass using a couple of raisins, then serve.

Yield:

Two servings

Nutritional info:

(per serving) Calories 204, Carbohydrates 45g, Protein 4g, Fat 3g, Fiber 9g, Sodium 266mg

CPSIA information can be obtained
at www.ICGtesting.com
Printed in the USA
LVHW081714030521
686340LV00033B/3557